Article 21

Adoption

A Commentary on the United Nations Convention
on the Rights of the Child

Editors

André Alen, Johan Vande Lanotte, Eugeen Verhellen,
Fiona Ang, Eva Berghmans and Mieke Verheyde

Article 21
Adoption

By

Sylvain Vité

Programme Manager, International Social Service/International Reference Centre
for the Rights of Children Deprived of their Family

Hervé Boéchat

Co-ordinator, International Social Service/International Reference Centre for the
Rights of Children Deprived of their Family

MARTINUS
NIJHOFF
PUBLISHERS

LEIDEN • BOSTON
2008

This book is printed on acid-free paper.

Library of Congress Cataloging-in-Publication Data

Vité, Sylvain.
   Article 21 : adoption / by Sylvain Vite, Herve Boechat.
      p. cm. — (A commentary on the United Nations Convention on the Rights of the Child, ISSN 1574-8626)
   Includes bibliographical references.
   ISBN 978-90-04-14874-1 (pbk. : acid-free paper) 1. Convention on the Rights of the Child (1989). Article 21. 2. Children (International law) 3. Children—Legal status, laws, etc. 4. Adoption—Law and legislation. I. Boechat, Herve. II. Convention on the Rights of the Child (1989). Article 21. French & English. III. Title.
   K639.A41989V58 2008
   341.4'8572—dc22

                                                                              2008019256

Cite as: S. Vité and H. Boéchat, "Article 21. Adoption", in: A. Alen, J. Vande Lanotte, E. Verhellen, F. Ang, E. Berghmans and M. Verheyde (Eds.) *A Commentary on the United Nations Convention on the Rights of the Child* (Martinus Nijhoff Publishers, Leiden, 2008).

ISSN 1574-8626
ISBN 978-90-04-14874-1

© 2008 by Koninklijke Brill NV, Leiden, The Netherlands.
Koninklijke Brill NV incorporates the imprints Brill, Hotei Publishers, IDC Publishers, Martinus Nijhoff Publishers and VSP.

Cover image by Nadia, 1 $^1/_2$ years old

http://www.brill.nl

PRINTED IN THE NETHERLANDS

CONTENTS

LIST OF ABBREVIATIONS

AAB	Accredited Adoption Body
CCPR	International Covenant on Civil and Political Rights
CESCR	International Covenant on Economic, Social and Cultural Rights
CRC	Convention on the Rights of the Child
CRC Committee	United Nations Committee on the Rights of the Child
ECHR	European Convention for the Protection of Human Rights and Fundamental Freedoms
ECtHR	European Court of Human Rights
ISS	International Social Service
NGO	Non-Governmental Organization
THC-1993	The Hague Convention on Protection of Children and Co-operation in Respect of Intercountry Adoption
1986 UN Declaration	1986 UN Declaration on Social and Legal Principles relating to the Protection and Welfare of Children, with Special Reference to Foster Placement and Adoption Nationally and Internationally
UNHCR	United Nations High Commissioner for Refugees
UNICEF	United Nations Children's Fund

AUTHOR BIOGRAPHY

Sylvain Vité obtained a postgraduate diploma in international relations at the Graduate Institute of International Studies (IUHEI) in 1993 and a Master of Law (LL.M) at the Washington College of Law in 1997. He completed his Ph.D in International Law at the University of Geneva in 1998. In 1991 he started working at the Constitutional Law Department of the University of Geneva, where he became a Lecturer in Comparative Constitutional Law and Legal Writing. From September 1999 to February 2001, he was a Delegate of the International Committee of the Red Cross, mainly in Colombia. He joined the World Organisation Against Torture upon his return in March 2001, where he focused on children's rights issues. He has been employed by the International Social Service since January 2005, first as Deputy Co-ordinator of the International Reference Centre for the Rights of Children Deprived of their Family (ISS/IRC), and then as Programme Manager. He is currently in charge of co-ordinating the drafting of the UN Guidelines for the protection and alternative care of children without parental care. In addition to this activity, he has also been a Senior Researcher and Lecturer at the University Centre for International Humanitarian Law since April 2002.

Hervé Boéchat is a Swiss lawyer currently working as Co-ordinator of the International Reference Centre for the Rights of Children Deprived of their Family (ISS/IRC). He obtained his Law degree from Neuchâtel University in 1995 and became a Solicitor in 1998. He carried out two field missions for the International Committee of the Red Cross in Afghanistan (2000) and Southern Sudan (2001). He was then employed as Scientific Collaborator at the Federal Office of Justice of Switzerland, in charge of the implementation of the Hague Convention on Protection of Children and Co-operation in respect of Intercountry Adoption, and the Hague Convention on the Civil Aspects of International Child Abduction. He completed a Master of Advanced Studies in Children's Rights in 2003 at Fribourg University, and published his research work about international adoption in 2006.

ACKNOWLEDGMENT

As both authors are collaborators at the General Secretariat of the International Social Service in Geneva (where the IRC program is run), parts of this contribution have been taken from various papers published by the IRC, such as editorials of the Monthly Review and position papers. The latter being the fruit of the work of the whole ISS/IRC team, the authors express to them their warm thanks. They are particularly grateful to Dr Isabelle Lammerant and Ms Christina Baglietto for their thorough review of this commentary.

Article 21

States Parties that recognize and/
or permit the system of adoption
shall ensure that the best interests
of the child shall be the paramount
consideration and they shall:
(a) Ensure that the adoption
of a child is authorized only
by competent authorities who
determine, in accordance with
applicable law and procedures
and on the basis of all pertinent
and reliable information, that the
adoption is permissible in view
of the child's status concerning
parents, relatives and legal
guardians and that, if required, the
persons concerned have given their
informed consent to the adoption on
the basis of such counselling as may
be necessary;

(b) Recognize that intercountry
adoption may be considered as an
alternative means of child's care,
if the child cannot be placed in
a foster or an adoptive family or
cannot in any suitable manner be
cared for in the child's country of
origin;

Article 21

Les Etats parties qui admettent et/
ou autorisent l'adoption s'assurent
que l'intérêt supérieur de l'enfant est
la considération primordiale en la
matière, et:
a) Veillent à ce que l'adoption
d'un enfant ne soit autorisée que
par les autorités compétentes, qui
vérifient, conformément à la loi et
aux procédures applicables et sur
la base de tous les renseignements
fiables relatifs au cas considéré,
que l'adoption peut avoir lieu eu
égard à la situation de l'enfant par
rapport à ses père et mère, parents
et représentants légaux et que, le cas
échéant, les personnes intéressées
ont donné leur consentement à
l'adoption en connaissance de cause,
après s'être entourées des avis
nécessaires;

b) Reconnaissent que l'adoption
à l'étranger peut être envisagée
comme un autre moyen d'assurer
les soins nécessaires à l'enfant, si
celui-ci ne peut, dans son pays
d'origine, être placé dans une famille
nourricière ou adoptive ou être
convenablement élevé;

(c) Ensure that the child concerned by inter-country adoption enjoys safeguards and standards equivalent to those existing in the case of national adoption;

(d) Take all appropriate measures to ensure that, in inter-country adoption, the placement does not result in improper financial gain for those involved in it;

(e) Promote, where appropriate, the objectives of the present article by concluding bilateral or multilateral arrangements or agreements, and endeavour, within this framework, to ensure that the placement of the child in another country is carried out by competent authorities or organs.

c) Veillent, en cas d'adoption à l'étranger, à ce que l'enfant ait le bénéfice de garanties et de normes équivalant à celles existant en cas d'adoption nationale;

d) Prennent toutes les mesures appropriées pour veiller à ce que, en cas d'adoption à l'étranger, le placement de l'enfant ne se traduise pas par un profit matériel indu pour les personnes qui en sont responsables;

e) Poursuivent les objectifs du présent article en concluant des arrangements ou des accords bilatéraux ou multilatéraux, selon les cas, et s'efforcent dans ce cadre de veiller à ce que les placements d'enfants à l'étranger soient effectués par des autorités ou des organes compétents.

CHAPTER ONE

INTRODUCTION*

1.1 *General Introduction*

1. When people speak about adoption, the image that first comes to mind is that of a child born in the third world, adopted by a couple living in the West, but one should keep in mind that adoption can be national (or domestic) too. Article 21 of the CRC makes reference to adoption in general in its first paragraph (sub-paragraph a), while sub-paragraphs b), c), d) and e) are more specifically dedicated to intercountry[1] adoption. The predominance of concerns related to intercountry adoption in Article 21 illustrates the fact that children's rights have to be protected in an intercountry adoption framework. However, intercountry adoption can not be considered separate from domestic adoption. The quantitative and qualitative development of the latter is, in point of fact, indispensable in assuring respect for the subsidiarity[2] of intercountry adoption.

2. Historically, adoption was used in Antiquity by the Greeks and Romans when, for instance, an Emperor wanted to choose a successor. In this case, adoption acted as an alternative means to create, by law or custom, a family tie between two non-related persons. From the Middle Ages onwards, most societies gave prominence to 'natural filiation', and adoption was limited to patrimonial purposes. It is mainly after the two World Wars that adoption resurfaced, as a way to create filiation ties in response to the numerous children orphaned by the conflicts. The evolution of Western societies then

---

* August 2006.
[1] Van Bueren explains that the term 'intercountry' as opposed to 'international' is used in order to avoid the impression given that there is a uniform type of adoption and that substantive rules exist which differ from national adoption., S. Detrick, *A commentary on the United Nations Convention on the Rights of the Child*, (The Hague, Martinus Nijhoff Publishers, 1999), p. 343. UNICEF-Innocenti Centre defines intercountry as an adoption involving the displacement of a child from his/her country of origin to the receiving country. International adoption refers to an adoption where adoptive parents and the child do not have the same nationality. UNICEF, *Innocenti Digest No. 4. Intercountry Adoption* (Florence, UNICEF ICDC, 1999), www.unicef-irc.org. In this contribution, 'intercountry' is used with reference to the CRC.
[2] *Cf. infra* No. 94.

paved the way for a new approach to adoption: progressively intercountry adoption became an answer to infertile couples, leading to a demand for children that has continuously increased since the seventies. Today, tens of thousands of children are adopted world-wide each year. For some years now, professionals and international institutions are concerned with the consequences of this substantial displacement of children population. For example, the fact that Western societies are so keen on adopting children from the third world has generated great pressure on the countries of origin. Today, it is common to analyse this situation in economical terms: since the demand is greater than the supply, exchanges can not be balanced. This leads to abuses by those who either want to benefit from the context financially, or those who are ready to pay to get a child in any way. In such a context, conditions are present to lead to any kind of excesses, including child trafficking.

3. From a sociological point of view the following elements[3] may play a role in sustaining the popularity of intercountry adoptions:

- Evolution of Western society: contraceptive methods, the heightened rate of infertility, and the reduced number of abandoned children have limited the opportunity for national adoptions;
- Social conception of family life: the importance of having children in order to be considered a family. This conception further leads to the 'right to a child concept' emerging in the eighties, which was then strongly denied by professionals and by the European Court of Human Rights;[4]
- New family models: the increasing acceptance of 'single parenthood' paved the way for single parent adoptions. Today, the question of conceding adoption to homosexual couples is being debated all over the Western world. Some legislators have already accepted it, such as in the Netherlands, Québec and Sweden;
- Influence of the media, particularly television: by broadcasting images of extreme poverty and disasters around the globe daily, the media is greatly contributing to creating a biased picture of the reality faced by developing countries. Western societies choose to focus on such aspects, without questioning whether or not those aspects are truly representative of what life is in those places. For instance, children living on the streets or in institutions are not necessarily abandoned, and are therefore not adoptable;
- Humanitarian consciousness: since the seventies a humanitarian spirit has emerged, developing new means of solidarity, thereby fostering the idea of a

---

[3] H. Boéchat, *Adoption internationale: une évolution entre éthique et marché* (Geneva, Edition de la Fondation Suisse du Service Social International, 2006), p. 23.
[4] *Cf. infra* No. 20.

global responsibility. In light of such a spirit, adoption may also be perceived as a way to help the most vulnerable.

4. Taking the above-mentioned elements into consideration, it is difficult to imagine that the demand for adopting foreign children will decrease at any time in the near future. However, what has been clearly demonstrated is the West's tendency to use intercountry adoption as an answer to the lack of children in Western societies, which is not at all the primary goal of this procedure! Intercountry adoption must be a measure to protect children who are faced with little or no opportunity in accessing a safe domestic environment within their countries of origin.

5. In order to steer the practice of intercountry adoption back onto the right path, international conventions outlined clear rules regarding the aims of intercountry adoption and the conditions under which it must be carried out. The two main texts are the Convention on the Rights of the Child (CRC) and the Hague Convention on Protection of Children and Co-operation in Respect of Intercountry Adoption (THC-1993).

1.2   Historical Background of Article 21 of the CRC

6. The first draft Convention on the Rights of the Child that Poland submitted to the UN Commission on Human Rights in a letter dated 17 January 1978 did not refer to adoption. The first mention of this issue was made by Barbados and Colombia in their respective comments on the Polish proposal. These two comments, which are at the origin of Article 21 of the CRC, read as follows:

> Barbados: 'It has been observed that no article deals directly with the adoption of children where this is desirable in their best interest. If this is to be accepted then provision should be made whereby an adoption should not take place without the consent of the parent. However such consent may be dispensed with by a competent court if the person whose consent is to be dispensed with: a) has abandoned, neglected or persistently ill-treated the infant; or b) cannot be found or is incapable of giving his consent or is withholding his consent unreasonably'.[5]

> Colombia: 'Having analysed articles I to X, we find that they reproduce the content of the ten articles of the Declaration of the Rights of the Child which

---

[5] *Travaux Préparatoires* (UN Doc. E/CN.4/1324), reproduced in United Nations Centre for Human Rights, *Legislative History of the Convention on the Rights of the Child (1978-1989), Article 21 (Adoption)*, (HR/1995/Ser.1/article 21), p. 5.

were adopted by the United Nations General Assembly in 1959, and to which the following might be added: 'a child who is adopted by nationals of a country other than his country of origin shall enjoy the same rights as are accorded to children of the country in which he is adopted'.[6]

7. Whereas the amendment proposed by Barbados dealt with adoption in general and formulated basic conditions for a child to be declared adoptable, the text elaborated by Colombia focused on intercountry adoption and the principle of non-discrimination. This dual approach was to be followed during the negotiation process and constitutes the general framework of Article 21 of the CRC's final version: general requirements for both domestic and intercountry adoption appear under letter (a) of this provision and specific standards related to intercountry adoption are included in letters (b) to (e). The Colombian paragraph on intercountry adoption was later developed on the basis of a proposal made by Norway, which suggested to include the State's responsibility to establish a child protection policy and legislation, the obligation to proceed through authorized agencies, the principle of non-discrimination between domestic and intercountry adoption, the validation of consents and proceedings in the countries involved and the right of the child to a name, nationality and legal guardian.[7]

1.3   The Hague Convention on Protection of Children and Co-operation in Respect of Intercountry Adoption

8. The Hague Convention on Protection of Children and Co-operation in Respect of Inter-country Adoption (THC-1993)[8] brought some substantial changes and improvements in the field of intercountry adoption. By putting the whole process under the scrutiny of the ratifying States' Central Authorities, THC-1993 has set up important safeguards and essential principles to be respected in order to guarantee, as much as possible, that intercountry adoption is in the best interests of the children concerned.

---

[6] *Travaux Préparatoires* (UN Doc. E/CN.4/1324/Add.2), reproduced in United Nations Centre for Human Rights, *o.c.* (note 5), p. 5.
[7] *Travaux Préparatoires* (UN Doc. E/CN.4/1982/30/Add.1, para. 77), reproduced in United Nations Centre for Human Rights, *o.c.* (note 5), p. 11.
[8] Hague Conference on Private International Law, Convention on Protection of Children and Co-operation in respect of Intercountry Adoption, adopted on 29 May 1993, entered into force on 1 May 1995, http://www.hcch.net/index_en.php?act=conventions.text&cid=69.

9. There are obvious links between Article 21 of the CRC and THC-1993 and their fundamental principles are mirroring one another. As the Hague Conference General Secretary states: 'The Hague Convention of 29 May 1993 comes within a broader legal scope which is essential to its understanding. The UN Convention on the Rights of the Child was a major source of inspiration for the authors of The Hague treaty. Although the latter keeps an autonomous feature with the CRC, it can be considered in many respects as an implementing instrument of the UN convention.'[9] Therefore, for a better understanding of Article 21 of the CRC, we will also refer in this contribution to THC-1993, its Articles as well as the numerous studies already carried out on issues regarding the treaty.

---

[9] J.H.A. van Loon, in: M.-F. Lücker-Babel, *Adoption internationale: comprendre les nouvelles normes* (Genève, Défense des Enfants-International, 1996), p. 3. For a discussion on this issue, see S. Dillon, 'Making Legal Regimes for Intercountry Adoption Reflect Human Rights Principles: Transforming the United Nations Convention on the Rights of the Child with the Hague Convention on Intercountry Adoption', *Boston University International Law Journal*, 21, 2003, pp. 212–215.

CHAPTER TWO

COMPARISON WITH RELATED INTERNATIONAL INSTRUMENTS

2.1 *Human and Children's Rights*

2.1.1 *UN Instruments on Children's and Human Rights*

a) *The UN Declaration on the Rights of the Child*
10. The *UN Declaration on the Rights of the Child*[10] of 20 November 1959 was a source of inspiration for the drafting of the UN Convention on the Rights of the Child. However, it does not contain any provision specifically dealing with child adoption. It provides that '[s]ociety and the public authorities shall have the duty to extend particular care to children without a family and to those without adequate means of support',[11] but it does not give further explanation on the forms of such care. Article 20(3) of the CRC develops this rule, stating that alternative care should include, among others, adoption.

b) *The UN Declaration on Social and Legal Principles Relating to the Protection and Welfare of Children, with Special Reference to Foster Placement and Adoption Nationally and Internationally*
11. One of the main mentions of child adoption in an international legal instrument appears in the 1986 *UN Declaration on Social and Legal Principles relating to the Protection and Welfare of Children, with special reference to Foster Placement and Adoption Nationally and Internationally* (1986 UN Declaration).[12] This text was partly at the origin of Article 21. It is divided in three parts: 1. General family and child welfare, 2. Foster placement, and 3. Adoption.

---

[10] United Nations, Declaration on the Rights of the Child, proclaimed by General Assembly resolution 1386 (XIV) of 20 November 1959, http://www.unhchr.ch/html/menu3/b/25.htm.
[11] *Ibid.*, principle 6.
[12] United Nations, Declaration on Social and Legal Principles relating to the Protection and Welfare of Children, with special reference to Foster Placement and Adoption Nationally and Internationally, proclaimed by General Assembly Resolution 41/85 of 3 December 1986, http://www.unhchr.ch/html/menu3/b/27.htm.

12. The first Chapter of this Declaration includes principles common to foster care and adoption. It provides that 'the first priority for a child is to be cared for by his/her own parents' (Art. 3). As a result, other forms of care, including adoption, are considered as subsidiary measures to parental care. This first part also includes the principle of the best interests of the child (Art. 5), the recognition that persons responsible for adoption procedures should have appropriate training (Art. 6), the child's right to a name, a nationality and a legal representative (Art. 8), and his/her need to know about his/her background (Art. 9).

13. The third Chapter of the Declaration focuses on adoption and makes a distinction between adoption in general (Arts. 13–16 and 19) and intercountry adoption (Arts. 17–18, 20–24). Some of these provisions were reproduced, and partly modified, in Article 21 of the CRC. This is the case, for example, of Articles 15 (adequate counselling to all persons concerned), 17 (subsidiarity of intercountry adoption), and 20 (competent authorities, non-discrimination, prohibition of improper financial gain). Other rules, on the contrary, do not explicitly appear in the text of Article 21. This does not mean however that they are not part of the international law of adoption. They provide further clarification on how the best interests of the child can be implemented in this context and should be considered, as such, as complementary recommendations to the prescriptions of Article 21 of the CRC. The 1986 UN Declaration states, for example, that States should assess the relationship of the child to be adopted and the prospective adoptive parents *prior* to the adoption and that the adopted child must enjoy all the rights resulting from being a full member of the adoptive family (Art. 16). It also provides that no intercountry adoption should take place before effective measures have been established to protect the children concerned (Art. 18). Other rules also deal with the prohibition of illicit placement (Art. 19), the nationality of the adopted child (Art. 22) or the legal validity of proceedings (Art. 23).

c) *Other Provisions of the CRC*
14. Since children without parental care and adopted children, like any other children, are entitled to enjoy all rights recognized by the CRC, Article 21 must be understood in relation to the other provisions of this instrument. In particular, the general principles underlying the CRC, such as the principle of non-discrimination (Art. 2), the best interests of the child (Art. 3), the right to life, survival and development (Art. 6), and the right to be heard (Art. 12), must be respected at all stages, when the adoption of a child

is envisaged. Moreover, the Convention recognizes the importance of the family 'as the fundamental group of society and the natural environment for the growth and well-being of all its members and particularly children [...]' and emphasizes its role 'for the full and harmonious development' of the child's personality.[13] This means that, in principle, parents share the primary responsibility for the upbringing and development of the child (Art. 18) and that children must not be separated from their parents against their will, except in exceptional circumstances and following a decision taken by competent authorities and subject to judicial review (Art. 9). Other relevant provisions include, among others, the right to acquire a nationality (Art. 7), the right to know and be cared for by his/her parents (Art. 7) and the States Parties' obligation to combat the illicit transfer and non-return of children abroad (Art. 11).

15. More specifically, Article 21 of the CRC is related to Article 20. The latter establishes the States Parties' responsibility to ensure alternative care for children temporarily or permanently deprived of their family. Article 20(3) further specifies that: 'Such care could include, inter alia, foster placement, kafalah of Islamic law, *adoption* or if necessary placement in suitable institutions for the care of children. When considering solutions, due regard shall be paid to the desirability of continuity in a child's upbringing and to the child's ethnic, religious, cultural and linguistic background.' Adoption under the Convention is therefore a possible alternative care measure among others. Where the reintegration of the child in his/her nuclear or extended family is not possible, a durable solution for the child should be secured without undue delay.

d) *Other UN Instruments*
16. At the universal level, Article 21, as well as Article 35 of the CRC on the 'prevention of the abduction of, the sale of or traffic in children for any purpose or in any form', was also completed by the *Optional Protocol to the Convention on the Rights of the Child on the sale of children, child prostitution and child pornography*.[14] This instrument requires States to criminalize any type of trafficking in children, including '[i]mproperly inducing consent, as an

---

[13] Preamble, paras. 6–7.
[14] United Nations, Optional Protocol to the Convention on the Rights of the Child on the Sale of Children, Child Prostitution and Child Pornography, adopted on 25 May 2000, entered into force on 18 January 2002, http://www.ohchr.org/english/law/crc-sale.htm.

intermediary, for the adoption of a child in violation of applicable international legal instruments on adoption.'[15]

17. Finally, the international instruments dealing with human rights in general are also relevant to define the rights of children concerned by adoption. Those include the *International Covenant on Civil and Political Rights* (CCPR)[16] and the *International Covenant on Economic, Social and Cultural Rights* (CESCR)[17] of 16 December 1966. Beside general provisions applicable to all human beings, both treaties contain articles dealing with children's rights.[18]

2.1.2 Regional Instruments on Children's and Human Rights

a) *Africa*

18. At regional level, the *African Charter on the Rights and Welfare of the Child* is the only convention which deals directly with child adoption.[19] Article 24 of the Charter reproduces word for word Article 21 of the CRC, adding, however, two clarifications and one new obligation.[20] Article 24(b) explicitly

---

[15] *Ibid.*, Arts. 2, 3 and 5.

[16] United Nations, International Covenant on Civil and Political Rights, adopted on 16 December 1966, entered into force on 23 March 1976, http://www.ohchr.org/english/law/ccpr.htm.

[17] United Nations, International Covenant on Economic, Social and Cultural Rights, adopted on 16 December 1966, entered into force on 3 January 1976, http://www.ohchr.org/english/law/cescr.htm.

[18] Art. 10(3) of the CESCR: 'Special measures of protection and assistance should be taken on behalf of all children and young persons without any discrimination for reasons of parentage or other conditions. Children and young persons should be protected from economic and social exploitation (...)'.

Art. 24 of the CCPR: '1. Every child shall have, without any discrimination as to race, colour, sex, language, religion, national or social origin, property or birth, the right to such measures of protection as are required by his status as a minor, on the part of his family, society and the State. 2. Every child shall be registered immediately after birth and shall have a name. 3. Every child has the right to acquire a nationality'.

The UN Human Rights Committee, commenting on Article 24 of the CCPR, recommended that States Parties, when presenting their periodic reports, should 'provide information on the special measures of protection adopted to protect children who are abandoned or deprived of their family environment in order to enable them to develop in conditions that most closely resemble those characterizing the family environment' (Human Rights Committee, *General Comment No. 17: Rights of the child (Art. 24)*, 7 April 1989, http://www.ohchr.org/english/bodies/hrc/comments.htm).

[19] African Union, African Charter on the Rights and Welfare of the Child, adopted on 11 July 1990, entered into force 29 November 1999, http://www.achpr.org/english/_info/child_en.html.

[20] Art. 24 of the Charter reads: 'State Parties which recognize the system of adoption shall ensure that the best interest of the child shall be the paramount consideration and they shall: (a) establish competent authorities to determine matters of adoption and ensure

states that intercountry adoption must be a measure of 'last resort', meaning that it must be authorized only when no other suitable care option is available in the child's country of origin. This principle, which establishes the 'subsidiarity' of intercountry adoption, is already contained in the CRC. The additional wording of the Charter thus emphasizes what already exists under the CRC. Also, Article 24(d) specifies that States Parties must fight not only against 'improper financial gain' in the process of intercountry adoption, but also against 'trafficking'. This also accentuates, in the context of intercountry adoption, an obligation already included in Article 35 of the CRC. Finally, the African Charter prescribes a new obligation: Article 24(f) obliges States Parties to 'establish a machinery to monitor the well-being of the adopted child'.

b) Americas

19. In the Americas, no specific convention deals with the human rights of children in case of adoption. The *American Convention on Human Rights* broadly states that '[e]very minor child has the right to the measures of protection required by his condition as a minor on the part of his family, society, and the state.'[21] However, when confronted with children's rights issues, the monitoring bodies of the American Convention refer to the CRC, including Article 21, to find a legal basis for their decisions, opinions or recommendations.[22] In its fifth report on the situation of human rights in Guatemala,

---

that the adoption is carried out in conformity with applicable laws and procedures and on the basis of all relevant and reliable information, that the adoption is permissible in view of the child's status concerning parents, relatives and guardians and that, if necessary, the appropriate persons concerned have given their informed consent to the adoption on the basis of appropriate counselling; (b) recognize that inter-country adoption in those States that have ratified or adhered to the International Convention on the Rights of the Child or this Charter, may, as the last resort, be considered as an alternative means of a child's care, if the child cannot be placed in a foster or an adoptive family or cannot in any suitable manner be cared for in the child's country of origin; (c) ensure that the child affected by inter-country adoption enjoys safeguards and standards equivalent to those existing in the case of national adoption; (d) take all appropriate measures to ensure that in inter-country adoption, the placement does not result in trafficking or improper financial gain for those who try to adopt a child; (e) promote, where appropriate, the objectives of this Article by concluding bilateral or multilateral arrangements or agreements, and endeavour, within this framework to ensure that the placement of the child in another country is carried out by competent authorities or organs; (f) establish a machinery to monitor the well-being of the adopted child'.

[21] Organization of American States, American Convention on Human Rights, adopted on 22 November 1969, entered into force on 18 July 1978, http://www.oas.org/juridico/english/Treaties/b-32.htm, Art. 19.

[22] See Inter-American Court of Human Rights, *Juridical Condition and Human Rights of the Child*, Advisory Opinion OC-17/02 of 28 August 2002, *Series A*, no. 17; Inter-American Court

for instance, the Inter-American Commission on Human Rights expressed concern regarding the severe deficiencies of the country's legislation on adoption. It thus stated that 'Guatemala [had] yet to adopt the necessary legislative and other measures to give full effect to its obligations under the Convention on the Rights of the Child, and the best interests of the child are not taken into account as a primary criterion in decision making.'[23]

c) *Europe*

20. Finally, European bodies concerned with the protection of human rights have also been confronted with adoption. The European Court of Human Rights (ECtHR) has dealt with such issues on the basis of Article 8 of the *European Convention for the Protection of Human Rights and Fundamental Freedoms* (ECHR), which establishes the right to respect for private and family life.[24] Within this framework, the Court has emphasized that 'although the right to adopt is not, as such, included among the rights guaranteed by the Convention, the relations between an adoptive parent and an adopted child are as a rule of the same nature as the family relations protected by Article 8 of the Convention.'[25] The Court also considered that the main international instruments on adoption must be used as legal references to give full effect to the European Convention on Human Rights on adoption issues. It has stated that '[w]ith regard in particular to the obligations imposed by Article 8 of the Convention on the Contracting States in the field of adoption, and to the effects of adoption on the relationship between adopters and those being adopted, they must be interpreted in the light of the Hague Conven-

---

of Human Rights, *Case of the 'Street Children', Villagrán-Morales et al.* v. *Guatemala*, Judgment of 19 November, 1999, *Series C*, no 63, in particular para. 194 *et seq.*

[23] Inter-American Commission on Human Rights, *Fifth Report on the Situation of Human Rights in Guatemala* (OEA/Ser.L/V/II.111, doc. 21 rev., 6 April 2001), Chapter XII: The Rights of the Child, para. 41.

[24] Council of Europe, European Convention for the Protection of Human Rights and Fundamental Freedoms, adopted on 4 November 1950, entered into force on 3 September 1953, http://conventions.coe.int/Treaty/en/Treaties/Html/005.htm.

Art. 8: '1. Everyone has the right to respect for his private and family life, his home and his correspondence. 2. There shall be no interference by a public authority with the exercise of this right except such as is in accordance with the law and is necessary in a democratic society in the interests of national security, public safety or the economic well-being of the country, for the prevention of disorder or crime, for the protection of health or morals, or for the protection of the rights and freedoms of others.'

[25] ECtHR, *Pini, Bertani, Manera and Atripaldi* v. *Romania*, Appl. No. 78028/01 and 78030/01, 22 June 2004, *Reports of Judgments and Decisions 2004-V (extracts)*, para. 140. See also ECtHR, *Fretté* v. *France*, Appl. No. 36515/97, 26 February 2002, *Reports of Judgments and Decisions 2002-I*, para. 32.

tion of 29 May 1993 on Protection of Children and Cooperation in respect of Intercountry Adoption, the United Nations Convention of 20 November 1989 on the Rights of the Child and the European Convention on the Adoption of Children, opened for signature in Strasbourg on 24 April 1967.'[26] The Court's decisions cover such questions as the right of the child to refuse his/her adoption,[27] the right of the birth parents to be heard before freeing their child for adoption,[28] the relationship between an unmarried father and his child placed for adoption by the mother,[29] or the situation of homosexual prospective adoptive parents.[30]

21. In addition, adoption issues may also be addressed by the Council of Europe Commissioner for Human Rights. In his assessment report on the situation in Romania, for example, while recognizing the progress made through the new legislation on adoption, he stated that 'international adoption should not be precluded if adoption is in the best interest of the child and is accompanied by all the guarantees which will enable the abuses of the past to be prevented.'[31]

22. The *European Convention on the Adoption of Children*, signed on 24 April 1967, aims to unify European principles and practices in the field of national adoption. This text is currently under review[32] by the Council of Europe and shall be replaced by the new European Convention on Adoption of Children.

23. Finally, at the European level, Recommendation 1443 (2000) 'International adoption: respecting children's rights', adopted by the European Parliamentary Assembly, is worth to be stressed as it entails strong statements such as: 'The Assembly therefore fiercely opposes the current transformation of international adoption into nothing short of a market regulated by the

---

[26] ECtHR, *Pini, Bertani, Manera and Atripaldi* v. *Romania, o.c.* (note 16), para. 139.

[27] *Ibid.*

[28] ECtHR, *P., C. and S.* v. *United Kingdom*, Appl. No. 56547/00, 16 July 2002, *Reports of Judgments and Decisions 2002-VI.*

[29] ECtHR, *Görgülü* v. *Germany*, Appl. No. 74969/01, 26 February 2004, http://www.echr.coe.int/echr/.

[30] ECtHR, *Fretté* v. *France, o.c.* (note 16). On the decisions of the European Court of Human Rights related to adoption, I. Lammerant, *L'adoption et les droits de l'homme en droit comparé* (Bruxelles, Bruylant, 2001), p. 35 *et seq.*

[31] Council of Europe Commissioner for Human Rights, *Follow up Report on Romania (2002–2005)*, Assessment of the progress made in implementing the recommendations of the Council of Europe Commissioner for Human Rights (CommDH(2006)7, 29 March 2006, Original: French), para. 32

[32] At the time this contribution is written, July 2006.

capitalist laws of supply and demand, and characterized by a one-way flow of children from poor states or states in transition to developed countries. It roundly condemns all crimes committed in order to facilitate adoption, as well as the commercial tendencies and practices that include the use of psychological or financial pressure on vulnerable families, the arranging of adoptions directly with families, the conceiving of children for adoption, the falsification of paternity documents and adoption via the Internet.'[33]

2.2   International Private Law

2.2.1   Overview

24. Intercountry adoptions were governed, for a long time, only by States' international private law. This led to very unsatisfactory situations as receiving States lacked information regarding the conditions under which the adoption took place in the countries of origin. Conversely, States of origin had limited information on the development of their children adopted abroad. A first attempt to regulate this situation was made by the Hague Conference in the 1960s, but with a mitigated success, as the *Convention on Jurisdiction, Applicable Law and Recognition of Decrees Relating to Adoptions*[34] (15 November 1965) has only been ratified by three countries.[35] The conclusion of the *Hague Convention on Protection of Children and Co-operation in respect of Intercountry Adoption*[36] in 1993 was therefore a great step forward. Mid 2006, the text had been ratified by 69 States, among which about 40 were countries of origin.

25. In this text, the definition of intercountry adoption in international law is based on the criteria of the usual residency, rather than the difference of citizenship between the child and the prospective adoptive parents. THC-1993 thus applies 'where a child habitually resident in one Contracting State ('the State of origin') has been, is being, or is to be moved to another Contracting State ('the receiving State') either after his or her adoption in

---

[33] Council of Europe, Parliamentary Assembly, *Recommendation 1443 (2000). International adoption: respecting children's rights*, 26 January 2000, http://assembly.coe.int/Mainf.asp?link=/Documents/AdoptedText/ta00/EREC1443.htm.

[34] Hague Conference on Private International Law, Convention on Jurisdiction, Applicable Law and Recognition of Decrees Relating to Adoptions, adopted on 15 November 1965, http://www.hcch.net/index_en.php?act=conventions.text&cid=75.

[35] Austria, Switzerland and United Kingdom. These three States denounced the convention after the ratification of THC-1993.

[36] *Cf. supra* (note 8).

the State of origin by spouses or a person habitually resident in the receiving State, or for the purposes of such an adoption in the receiving State or in the State of origin.'[37] In addition, adoption is characterized by the permanency of the relationship created.[38]

26. In the American continent, the *Inter-American Convention on Conflict of Laws Concerning the Adoption of Minors* (24 May 1984) governs intercountry adoptions among 13 States,[39] setting international private law rules based on the criteria of the habitual residence of the child.[40] Also, the Organization of American States adopted a resolution on 7 June 1999 called 'Strengthening of National Systems and International Cooperation in the Area of International Adoptions' which recalls the fundamental principles intercountry adoptions shall respect.[41]

2.2.2 Main Types of Adoption

27. From a legal perspective, one generally considers that there are two main types of adoption, known as full adoption and simple adoption. Given that domestic and intercountry adoptions have assumed such proportions and are increasingly scrutinized by the international community, legislators and adoption professionals frequently question the legal and social consequences of these two institutions. If debates are kept fuelled, it is due, in particular, to the fact that the distinction between simple and full adoption is characterized by a lack of coherence, both in its defining criteria and when it comes to possible conversions under national law.

---

[37] Article 2(1) of THC-1993.

[38] Article 2(2) of THC-1993 provides that '[t]he Convention covers only adoptions which create a permanent parent-child relationship.' Temporary forms of care are not covered by Article 21 of the CRC, but other provisions of the CRC are relevant in these situations, in particular Articles 3 and 20 of the CRC.

[39] Belize, Bolivia, Brazil, Chile, Colombia, Dominican Republic, Ecuador, Haiti, Mexico, Panama, Paraguay, Uruguay and Venezuela.

[40] Organization of American States, Inter-American Convention on Conflict of Laws Concerning the Adoption of Minors, adopted on 24 May 1984, entered into force on 26 May 1988, http://www.oas.org/juridico/english/Sigs/b-48.html.

[41] Organization of American States, General Assembly, Resolution 1632 (XXIX-O/99). Strengthening of National Systems and International Cooperation in the Area of International Adoptions, 7 June 1999, http://www.oas.org/juridico/english/ga-res99/eres1632.htm.

a) *Full Versus Simple Adoption*

28. The criteria for defining simple and full adoption vary according to cultural origins, the socio-political context and the concept of the family in each country under review. This diversity frequently gives rise to complications amongst jurisdictions over the effects and the recognition of these adoptions.

Simple adoption and full adoption can be differentiated in accordance with several criteria, of which the two main ones upheld by current doctrine are, either the severance or the maintenance of the ties of legal filiation with the family of origin, or the revocability or irrevocability of the adoption order.

29. The first criterion (founded upon the ties of legal filiation) is based, on the one hand, on the full integration of the child in the extended adoptive family and the severance of ties with the family of origin in the context of full adoption. On the other hand, simple adoption maintains the legal bond with the family of origin and establishes only a limited adoptive parental relationship between the adopters and the adoptee.

30. A second way of differentiating between the two types of adoption is to envisage the adoption order from the perspective of its potential revocability: if it is irrevocable, then the adoption is considered full. Otherwise, if it is revocable, it will be considered simple. This is mainly the approach taken by French law. An analysis of comparative law shows the existence of systems in which the two types of criteria coexist, the one severing the ties with the family of origin and the other maintaining them, but both being revocable. The criterion of revocability does not, therefore, make it possible in this case to distinguish between full and simple adoption.

31. National legislation only rarely mentions explicitly if adoption, as conceived in the country, falls under simple or full adoption; thus, the recognition of one type of adoption is often based upon a case-by-case interpretation of the texts in force.

b) *Interests of Simple or Full Adoption*

32. Full adoption has often aroused the interest of national legislators thanks to its key role in family integration. Since the child is totally and exclusively integrated in the extended adoptive family, this type of adoption offers greater legal and affective stability. Despite criticisms and worries about the effects of severance, sometimes considered too final, full adoption has become the rule in a large number of Western countries.

33. Simple adoption, on the other hand, allows for the coexistence of two parallel lines of filiation. It establishes a tie of legal filiation between adopters and adoptees while maintaining the existence of legal ties to the family of origin. This possibility may attract those who cannot imagine a total breach between the parents of origin and the child as is often the case in many countries in Africa and Asia.

34. In Western countries, these arguments would explain the growing preference for full adoption as the general rule, with the possibility of limiting simple adoption to more exceptional and complex cases, such as step-child adoption or open adoption.[42]

c) *Recognition and Conversion of Intercountry Adoption*
35. If the distinction between simple and full adoption is already difficult under national law, recognising these when facing intercountry adoptions is all the more complex. In practice, it is common to convert a simple adoption of the country of origin into a full adoption in the receiving country. The conversion in itself raises no legal issues, since it is provided for in THC-1993 (Articles 23–27). Nonetheless, the conditions of conversion and, sometimes, their lack of implementation, are sources of ethical problems. In fact, THC-1993 requires that 'where an adoption granted in the State of origin does not have the effect of terminating a pre-existing legal parent-child relationship, it may, in the receiving State which recognizes the adoption under the Convention, be converted into an adoption having such an effect if the law of the receiving State so permits and if the consents (...) have been given or are given for the purpose of such an adoption' (Article 27). That means that the parents or guardians who have given their initial consent to a simple adoption should also give it to a full adoption and its effects. It would therefore be necessary to consult, once again, the people concerned so as to ensure that they henceforth consent to a complete and permanent severance of the ties of legal filiation between the child and the family of origin. Nonetheless, given the practical difficulties, these conditions of conversion are unfortunately only rarely complied with.

---

[42] Some countries of the Anglo-Saxon legal tradition have introduced in their legislation the so-called open adoption. In brief, it refers to a full adoption which allows for an informal relationship between the child, the adoptive family and the family of origin. The biological parents and the child thus maintain an emotional relationship before and after adoption, within a framework formally defined by a contract between the parties and supported by the competent social services.

36. The distinction between simple and full adoption raises questions that go beyond the simple definition of the concept, including ethical concerns that must be taken into account at the time of any conversion of a foreign adoption. If conditions are such that legal requirements can only be implemented with difficulty, the conversion of simple adoptions into full adoptions should only be limited to some very specific circumstances, for example, when the parents are unable to give their consent or are unknown.

CHAPTER THREE

ANALYSIS OF ARTICLE 21

3.1 Scope of Article 21 (Art. 21, Introductory Sentence)

3.1.1 Definitions

37. As the word 'adoption' covers a great variety of legal approaches, customs and practices around the world, it would be very difficult to give a definition which encompasses all of them. In particular, the traditional kinship care and foster care existing in many countries raises specific problems as it may not fall under any formal control, even though the status of the fostered child is sometimes very close to that of the adoptee. 'There is a rich variety of social functions performed by adoption in non-literate societies and, as a result, its conditions, procedure and effects also vary immensely.'[43] For the purpose of this contribution, adoption is understood in its more widely known sense as a social and legal practice through which a person acquires new family ties that are defined as equivalent to biological ties and which supersede the old ones, either wholly or in part.[44]

3.1.2 States Parties that Recognize and/or Permit the System of Adoption

a) *Historical Background*
38. Article 21 of the CRC does not apply to all States Parties to the CRC, but is limited to those countries that 'recognize and/or permit the system of adoption.' This introductive paragraph was added during the negotiations as a response to an intervention from the delegate of Bangladesh, who reminded the participants that this provision was 'liable to give difficulties in Muslim countries since the understanding of Bangladesh [was] that adoption is not a recognized institution under Muslim law.' The delegate added

---

[43] J.H.A. van Loon, 'International co-operation and protection of children with regards to intercountry adoption', *RCADI* 244, 1993–VII, p. 207.
[44] Definition partly based on J.H.A. van Loon, *l.c.* (note 1), p. 206.

that the recognition of adoption would raise complex problems regarding, in particular, inheritance rights in Islamic jurisdictions.[45]

39. This concern was shared by the Libyan Arab Jamahiriya, whose representative stated, during the second reading of Article 21, that adoption conflicts with 'one of the imperative principles of the Islamic Shari'a.'[46] Accordingly, he proposed either to give up including an Article on adoption in the Convention, leaving interested States to regulate this issue through bilateral or multilateral agreements, or to insert a saving clause in this provision. With respect to the second solution, he also proposed 'the inclusion of a stipulation confining the application of this Article to the States that recognize or permit the practice of adoption.'[47] This formula was finally adopted, in a slightly modified version, as the final text of the Article.

40. Despite this amendment, several States, which do not authorize adoption, explicitly made a reservation to Article 21 of the CRC. These States include Bangladesh, Brunei Darussalam, Egypt, Indonesia, Jordan, Kuwait, the Maldives, Oman, Syria and the United Arab Emirates.[48] However, these reservations are superfluous, since the introductory part of Article 21 already makes clear that this provision does not apply to these countries. This is why the CRC Committee has recommended them to withdraw their reservations.[49]

41. The applicability of Article 21 of the CRC was also questioned in the case of traditional forms of adoption. Canada made a reservation in this regard, stating that it would not apply this provision to the extent that it may be inconsistent 'with customary forms of care among aboriginal people.'[50] However, the CRC Committee considered that the Convention must apply to all

---

[45] *Travaux Préparatoires* (UN Doc. E/CN.4/1986/39), Annex IV, reproduced in United Nations Centre for Human Rights, *o.c.* (note 5), p. 16.

[46] *Travaux Préparatoires* (UN Doc. E/CN.4/1989/WG.1/WP.3), reproduced in United Nations Centre for Human Rights, *o.c.* (note 5), p. 20.

[47] *Ibid.* See also, the intervention of Egypt, *Travaux Préparatoires, Report of the Working Group to the Commission on Human Rights* (UN Doc. E/CN.4/1989/48), reproduced in United Nations Centre for Human Rights, *o.c.* (note 5), pp. 22 and 24, paras. 16 and 350.

[48] UN Treaty Collection, *Reservations and Declarations to the UN Convention on the Rights of the Child*, http://www.unhchr.ch/html/menu3/b/treaty15_asp.htm.

[49] See, for instance, CRC Committee, *Concluding Observations: Jordan* (UN Doc. CRC/C/15/ Add.125, 2000), paras. 10–11; *Egypt* (CRC/C/15/Add.145, 2001), paras. 9–10.

[50] UN Treaty Collection, *o.c.* (note 48).

forms of adoption and therefore recommended Canada to withdraw its reservation.[51]

b) *Islamic Law*

42. States which operate in accordance with Islamic law do not recognize adoption, as they consider that filiation can only be based on blood ties. Instead, such countries may foresee some other means for a family to take care of a child which is not theirs biologically, the most common being the 'kafalah' – a permanent form of family foster care (mentioned in Article 20 of the CRC). Its specificities may vary from one country to another, but in general, foster parents have an obligation of maintenance towards the child, while the latter usually does not bear the foster family's name and has no right to inheritance. Also, some Islamic countries, where the system of personal religious laws is followed, may allow non-Muslim people to adopt under specific laws.

43. Considering that intercountry adoption is more and more 'globalized', it becomes frequent for prospective adoptive parents to look for children in countries whose laws only recognize *kafalah*. This raises very difficult questions, from the international private law perspective as well as from the ethical point of view. Answers are diverse, depending on the country of origin and the receiving country involved.

c) *Countries Where Full Adoption Does Not Exist*

44. Traditions and judicial systems in some countries, especially in Asia, do not foresee the legal institution of full adoption as an artificial creation of family ties. If traditional foster care or kinship care does exist, it often does not modify the original family ties: an adoption may have the effects of a simple adoption towards the family of origin as it maintains the filiation ties. But it may also have, at the same time, the effects of a full adoption vis-à-vis the adoptive family, given that the child benefits from the same rights as a natural child. This particular view exists, for instance, in Vietnam.[52]

---

[51] CRC Committee, *Concluding Observations: Canada* (CRC/C/15/Add.37, 1995), paras. 10 and 18.

[52] 'In Vietnamese law, the status of adoptive filiation is assimilated with a blood relationship. In the adoptive family, the adopted child has the same rights and obligations as a legitimate child. The adopter enjoys all the parental authority rights. There aren't any different types of adoption in Vietnamese law as there may exist in other countries, such as in France where the law distinguishes between simple and full adoption. According to Vietnamese law, adoption does not break the pre-existing filiation bond of the adoptee. Therefore, the adoptee keeps all his/her rights in his/her family of origin, including succession rights.

Therefore, one could question the validity of the 'conversion' of a decision entrusting a child to an adoptive family while the country of origin's legislation does not foresee the same consequences as the ones that will follow the adoption pronounced in the receiving country.[53]

3.2   The Best Interests of the Child (Art. 21, Introductory Sentence)

3.2.1   Historical Background

45. The principle of the best interests of the child was first mentioned during the drafting process of Article 21 of the CRC, not as a legal reference that must prevail in each step of the adoption procedure, but as a source and justification for international law developments on this issue. Barbados, in its initial proposal, argued that the best interests of the child required that the CRC established a legal framework for adoption.[54]

46. The insertion of this principle in the Article itself was actually an initiative of the Argentine, French and Norwegian delegations, which had received the task of drafting a compromise text on intercountry adoption. They suggested that States Parties would have to take 'all necessary measures to secure the best interests of the child who is the subject of intercountry adoption'.[55] It was deemed, however, that this principle was of general application, and should not be limited to intercountry adoption only. The reference to this principle was thus moved to the introductory phrase during the second reading of Article 21.[56] The principle of the best interests of the child would thus apply both to domestic and intercountry adoptions.

47. However, some delegations expressed their concern that a simple reference to the 'best interests of the child' would allow for the other interests –

The adoptee bears the name of his/her biological parents and the first name the latter has given to him/her. However, the adoptee may ask the competent authority to change his/her first and last name.' Van Binh Nguyen, 'Le droit et la pratique de l'adoption internationale au Vietnam', in: Assocation Louis Chatin, L'adoption internationale en droit comparé; Actes du colloque, 25–26 April 2003 (unofficial translation).

[53] Cf supra Nos. 35–36.

[54] Travaux Préparatoires (UN Doc. E/CN.4/1324), reproduced in United Nations Centre for Human Rights, o.c. (note 5), p. 5.

[55] Travaux Préparatoires, Report of the Working Group to the Commission on Human Rights (UN Doc. E/CN.4/1982/30/Add.1), reproduced in United Nations Centre for Human Rights, o.c. (note 5), p. 12, para. 78.

[56] Travaux Préparatoires (UN Doc. E/CN.4/1989/48), reproduced in United Nations Centre for Human Rights, o.c. (note 5), p. 23, para. 349.

including the child's parents' interests – to interfere in the adoption process. Based on an initial proposal by the Netherlands, the delegation of Norway suggested to solve this problem by specifying that the best interests of the child must be 'the paramount consideration'.[57] The introductory phrase was finally adopted by consensus.

48. Other issues related to the best interests of the child in adoption procedures were debated during the drafting of the Convention. In the revised version of the draft text presented in 1978 by Poland, it was proposed that the States Parties undertake measures so as 'to facilitate adoption of children.'[58] This initial proposal however was not approved by the Working Group. Even a modification suggested by Australia, whereby adoption would be facilitated only 'where appropriate',[59] was not kept and the text was finally deleted in the final version. Therefore, it may be considered that the CRC is not aimed at 'facilitating' adoption, but rather at ensuring that each child deprived of parental care may enjoy the most appropriate measures of care and protection. Among these measures, adoption should be made available to the child, as it ensures permanency through the creation of new filiation ties.

49. The issue of confidentiality of adoption records was also largely debated during the drafting process of Article 21 of the CRC. The United States proposed that access to such records should only be permitted 'by judicial order in accordance with applicable law and procedures.'[60] This proposal however raised resistance from various delegations, arguing that this would lead to implementation problems in practice and that confidentiality was an issue of family privacy, rather than of children's rights.[61] Finally, the United States decided to withdraw its initiative, explaining that the draft Article was neutral on this point and at least did not require the disclosure of adoption records.[62]

---

[57] *Travaux Préparatoires* (UN Doc. E/CN.4/1989/48), reproduced in United Nations Centre for Human Rights, *o.c.* (note 5), p. 25 *et seq.*, paras. 359–364.

[58] *Travaux Préparatoires* (UN Doc. E/CN.4/1349), reproduced in United Nations Centre for Human Rights, *o.c.* (note 5), p. 6.

[59] *Travaux Préparatoires* (UN Doc. E/CN.4/1475), reproduced in United Nations Centre for Human Rights, *o.c.* (note 5), p. 7.

[60] *Travaux Préparatoires* (UN Doc. E/CN.4/1982/30/Add.1), reproduced in United Nations Centre for Human Rights, *o.c.* (note 5), p. 14, para. 88.

[61] *Ibid.*, para. 89.

[62] *Travaux Préparatoires* (UN Doc. E/CN.4/1986/39), reproduced in United Nations Centre for Human Rights, *o.c.* (note 5), p. 16, para. 12.

3.2.2 *Implications*

50. Article 21 reproduces the general principle of Article 3(1) of the CRC within the framework of its specific scope of application. It provides that 'the system of adoption shall ensure that the best interests of the child shall be the paramount consideration.' It is also directly inspired by Article 5 of the 1986 UN Declaration, which establishes that '[i]n all matters relating to the placement of a child outside the care of the child's own parents, the best interests of the child, particularly his or her need for affection and right to security and continuing care, should be the paramount consideration.' Contrary to the above mentioned Article 5, Article 21 of the CRC is clearly binding for States Parties: it is part of a Convention (and not a Declaration) and provides that the best interests of the child 'shall' (and not only 'should') be the paramount consideration. This means that the child's interests must take precedence over any other interests,[63] in particular those of his/her birth parents, prospective adoptive parents, accredited adoption bodies (AABs) or the States concerned. This principle must be respected in any decision throughout the adoption process, from the separation of the child from his/her parents until follow-up measures once the adoption is pronounced. It has to be stressed too, that this is the only place in the CRC where the best interests of the child are 'the', and not 'a', primary consideration.[64]

51. In the field of both domestic and intercountry adoption, this principle lies at the heart of the norms that govern it: the CRC (Art. 21) and THC-1993 (Art. 1 a), Art. 4 b), Art. 16 (1) d))[65] emphasize it specifically. THC-1993 refers notably, in its Preamble, to the CRC, which provides that States have a particular duty to protect children deprived of parental care (Arts. 20 and 21). An important element in achieving this is permanency

---

[63] R. Hodgkin and P. Newell, *Implementation Handbook for the Convention on the Rights of the Child*, second edition (New York, UNICEF, 2002), p. 296.

[64] UNICEF, *Innocenti Digest No. 4. Intercountry Adoption*, o.c. (note 1), p. 5.

[65] Art. 1 a) of THC-1993: 'The objects of the present Convention are to establish safeguards to ensure that intercountry adoptions take place in the best interests of the child and with respect for his or her fundamental rights as recognized in international law.'

Art. 4 b) of THC-1993: 'An adoption within the scope of the Convention shall take place only if the competent authorities of the State of origin have determined, after possibilities for placement of the child within the State of origin have been given due consideration, that an intercountry adoption is in the child's best interests.'

Art. 16(1) d) of THC-1993: 'If the Central Authority of the State of origin is satisfied that the child is adoptable, it shall determine, on the basis in particular of the reports relating to the child and the prospective adoptive parents, whether the envisaged placement is in the best interests of the child.'

planning, that is to say the devising for every child in care of a permanent, and preferably family, protective solution, including intercountry adoption when no adoptive family can be found in the country of origin.

52. The European Court of Human Rights has stressed that the best interests of the child have to be defined by the authorities of the child's country of habitual residence. The decision of adoption has to be proportionate and has to safeguard procedural measures guaranteeing the respect of family life.[66]

53. This principle entails a case by case appreciation of the child's best interests, and opposes itself to a general approach that would consider adoption as the best solution whenever parents are not able or willing to care for their child. As a basic rule, the CRC insists on the role and responsibility of the child's parents in his/her upbringing. It establishes a 'presumption [...] that the children's best interests are served by being with their parents wherever possible.'[67] Therefore adoption should be envisaged only when all efforts aimed at enabling the child to remain in or return to the care of his/her parents have proved inefficient.[68] Together with legislation on adoption, governments should develop and implement policies designed to support family preservation. According to the CRC Committee, such policies should address the difficulties that some parents and families encounter, such as 'unemployment, malnutrition and lack of adequate housing – which may cause abandonment or abuse resulting in placement of children in institutions or in adoption.'[69]

54. This 'paramount consideration' emphasizes the importance of putting the child and his/her needs at the centre of all decisions which concern him/her. It is up to the authorities in charge to make sure that this principle is respected, in particular, in cases of intercountry adoption, by the authorities foreseen by Articles 4 (adoptability), 5 (eligibility and suitability of prospective adoptive parents) and 16 (matching) of THC-1993. As stated by the European Court of Human Rights, '[a]doption means "providing a child with a family, not a family with a child", and the State must see to it that the

---

[66] European Commission of Human Rights, *X v. France*, Appl. No. 9993/82, 5 December 1982, DR 31, p. 241. See U. Kilkelly, *The Child and the European Convention on Human Rights* (Dartmouth, Ashgate, 1999), p. 298.

[67] R. Hodgkin and P. Newell, *o.c.* (note 21), p. 297. See Arts. 5, 7, 9, and 18 of the CRC.

[68] See CRC Committee, *Day of General Discussion on Children Without Parental Care: Recommendations* (UN Doc. CRC/C/153, 2006); CRC Committee, *Concluding Observations: Nicaragua* (UN Doc. CRC/C/15/Add.265, 2005), para. 39.

[69] *Ibid.*, para. 38.

persons chosen to adopt are those who can offer the child the most suitable home in every respect.'[70]

55. In *Pini et al.* v. *Romania*, the European Court considered, for example, that the interests of two girls, who had consistently objected to their adoption by an Italian couple, should prevail over the interests of the prospective adoptive parents to create a new family with the children. In this regard, the Court stated that '[t]here are unquestionably no grounds, from the children's perspective, for creating emotional ties against their will between them and people to whom they are not biologically related and whom they view as strangers. It is clear from the facts of the case that at present Florentina and Mariana would rather remain in the social and family environment in which they have grown up [...], into which they consider themselves to be fully integrated and which is conducive to their physical, emotional, educational and social development, than be transferred to different surroundings abroad.'[71]

56. However, the best interests of the child is not the unique consideration to take into account in the adoption process. This principle must be defined in accordance with other rights which have to be safeguarded, such as the rights of the child not to be arbitrarily separated from his/her parents and to be raised by them,[72] or the right of biological parents to have their family life preserved, in cases where, for instance, their consent was not adequately given.[73] The interests of the child should not be separated from the interests of his/her birth or adoptive family. The interests of the child and his/her family cannot be dissociated. 'To ignore the family is to amputate the child'[74] and 'to focus on the child only is to ignore him as a subject person.'[75] Or, as stated in Article 2 of the 1986 UN Declaration, 'child welfare depends upon good family welfare.' D. Manai[76] wrote: 'The child, an incomplete and evolving being, is not an ordinary right holder. He is ambivalent. Therefore the

---

[70] ECtHR, *Fretté* v. *France*, o.c. (note 25), para. 42. See also ECtHR, *Pini, Bertani, Manera and Atripaldi* v. *Romania*, o.c. (note 25), para. 156.

[71] Ibid., para. 153 *et seq.*

[72] Art. 9 of the CRC and Art. 8 of the ECHR.

[73] I. Lammerant gives the example of a decision taken by Italian justice where a child from the Philippines was removed from an adoptive family which had adopted him fraudulently. I. Lammerant, o.c. (note 30), p. 46.

[74] P. Verdier, *L'enfant en miettes* (Toulouse, Privat, 1978), p. 124.

[75] M. Manoni mentioned by P. Verdier, *L'adoption aujourd'hui* (Paris, Paidos/Le Centurion, 1985), p. 146.

[76] D. Manai, 'La dispense de consentement en matière d'adoption: autonomie individuelle et contrôle social', *Déviance et Société*, No. 3, 1990, pp. 275–294, specifically pp. 292–293.

concept of the child's interest cannot be defined as such, since it cannot be classified as a legal autonomous category; it is dependent and subordinate. It can only be apprehended within the relation of the child with his birth parents or with the adopters.' In addition, 'it is the nature of the relation which defines the interest of the child.'[77]

57. Transposed on a more global level, the best interest of the child, in the framework of intercountry adoption, also means that the propositions of adoptable children by countries of origin should be given priority over the requests of receiving countries. Therefore, in order to be really focused on the child, and not on the adopters, and as a way to try to diminish the discrepancy between the wishes of prospective adoptive parents and the needs of countries of origin, adoption should result in the despatch of the files of children in need of intercountry adoption by the States of origin to the potential receiving States, and not – as is more often the case at present – in the despatch by the receiving countries to the countries of origin of a great number of files of prospective adopters requesting the profiles of children who do not necessarily need a foreign family. In Porto Alegre (Brazil), for example, the reversal of the procedure (in other words the flow of files) has been implemented. The Authorities are no longer drowning in files of prospective adopters who do not take kindly to being kept waiting. They can, in collaboration with their partners in the receiving States, devote themselves to their priority mission, namely the search for a family for each child who needs one, including children who are difficult to place.[78]

58. One also has to keep in mind that the best interest of the child may be perceived in a different manner according to different cultures. Its respect does not necessarily lead to the same answers as the ones commonly admitted in Western societies. As mentioned before, Islamic law only recognizes biological filiation, and therefore gives preference to family foster care (such as *kafalah*).

---

[77] See also F. Tulkens, 'Le placement des mineurs et le droit au respect de la vie familiale (Observations on the Andersson case, European Court on Human Rights, 25th February 1992)', *Revue Trimestrielle des Droits de l'Homme*, 1993, pp. 557–573, specifically p. 564.
[78] Editorial of the ISS/IRC Monthly Review, n° 65, March 2004, p. 2.

3.3   Permissibility of Adoption (Art. 21, para. a)

3.3.1   Historical Background

59. Article 21 of the CRC provides that States Parties bear the responsibility of determining that each adoption is 'permissible'. This obligation was first introduced in 1981 by the delegation of Denmark, which proposed to add to the draft Article the following sentence: 'The child shall not [...] be adopted unless there has been a serious attempt to investigate and elucidate his status concerning parents, guardians, relatives and other biological and stable social relations.'[79] The delegation of the United States proposed later to detail this requirement by adding two main amendments: first, that 'pertinent and reliable evidence' had to demonstrate that the child was 'legally available for adoption'; second, that the biological parents had to receive 'sufficient counselling' for them to be able to take an informed decision.[80] France, however, considered that requiring 'evidence' was inappropriate in this framework and suggested that this word be replaced by the word 'information.'

60. Following a meeting of Non-Governmental Organizations (NGOs), which took place in Buenos Aires, the government of Argentina also submitted an amendment according to which the adoption process had to be based on decisions taking the child's view into consideration.[81] This text was not endorsed by the Working Group, but the concern raised by Argentina was dealt with under Article 12 of the CRC. This provision obliges States Parties to 'assure to the child who is capable of forming his or her own views the right to express those views freely in all matters affecting the child, the views of the child being given due weight in accordance with the age and maturity of the child' (Art. 12(1) of the CRC).

61. The need for the intervention of competent authorities in the adoption process was partly mentioned in the initial draft Article submitted by Barbados. However, this text was limited in scope. It only provided that the lack of consent by the birth parents to the adoption of their child could be superseded, under certain circumstances, by 'a competent court.' A broader

---

[79] *Travaux Préparatoires* (UN Doc. E/CN.4/1475), reproduced in United Nations Centre for Human Rights, *o.c.* (note 5), p. 7, para. 289.

[80] *Travaux Préparatoires* (UN Doc. E/CN.4/1982/30/Add.1), reproduced in United Nations Centre for Human Rights, *o.c.* (note 5), p. 10, para. 73.

[81] *Travaux Préparatoires* (UN Doc. E/CN.4/1989/WG.1/WP.1); reproduced in United Nations Centre for Human Rights, *o.c.* (note 5), p. 22.

approach was then proposed by a group of NGOs. A new paragraph was thus submitted, according to which 'adoption can only be decided by a competent body set up in accordance with principles of national law.'[82] This proposal, after being redrafted, was included in the final version of Article 21, both in paragraph a) on adoption in general and in the part dedicated more specifically to intercountry adoption. Paragraph e) provides that, when States Parties decide to regulate adoption through bilateral or multilateral arrangements or agreements, they must ensure that 'the placement of a child in another country is carried out by competent authorities or organs.'

3.3.2   Competent Authorities

62. Article 21 para. a) of the CRC, provides that the adoption of a child is permissible only when authorized by 'competent authorities'. Implementing the CRC therefore asks for important institutional developments. It is perhaps one of the most crucial aspects of the process, considering the vast range of issues, including budgetary issues.

a) *Notion of 'Competent'*
63. The handling of a child's case cannot be left to the birth parents, to prospective adoptive parents, to unqualified protagonists or those of doubtful ethics. It must be carried out by services competent in child protection, which, as far as possible, should be pluridisciplinary and subject to accreditation and periodic inspection by competent national authorities. Decisions related to adoptions will have to be taken preferably by collegiate bodies whose different members have diverse and complementary professions and experiences at their disposal. As recommended by the CRC Committee, these authorities should be adequately trained to be able to fulfil their responsibilities.[83] In any case the decisions should be based on technical reports prepared by appropriate specialists (social workers, psychologists, medical doctors, lawyers, *etc.*). The proceedings must be carried out by public authorities, whether administrative or judicial, in accordance with the legislation of each country. These proceedings must be endowed with adequate procedural guarantees for the people concerned and especially for the child who must be heard and must have his/her opinions taken into

---

[82] *Travaux Préparatoires* (UN Doc. E/CN.4/1982/WG.1/WP.1), reproduced in United Nations Centre for Human Rights, *o.c.* (note 5), p. 8, para. 4.
[83] CRC Committee, *Concluding Observations: Panama* (UN Doc. CRC/C/15/Add.68, 1997), para. 31.

account whenever possible. In particularly difficult situations, the child may need individual assistance (by a social worker, lawyer, government ministry) during the proceedings.

64. Professionals engaged in adoption proceedings should be guided as a priority, in the perception of their work and in their practice, by the needs and rights of the child. While they must be careful to listen to the demands of birth parents and to take into consideration the wishes of prospective adoptive parents, they are not required to accord them priority, but rather to consider the extent to which they correspond to the best interests of the child. Professionals must be aware that an adoption in the best interests of the child is one that fosters the creation of an environment or family relationship that satisfy all parties at best.

b) *Accredited Adoption Bodies in Intercountry Adoption*
65. On several occasions, the CRC Committee expressed its concern regarding intercountry adoptions which are not carried out through competent authorities or accredited adoption bodies,[84] but rather through individual channels, resulting in the risk of increasing sales of children.[85] According to the Committee, prospective adoptive parents should not be allowed to select the child they will adopt.[86] When such bodies are established, States Parties should also develop control systems. For example, the Committee criticized the Russian Federation for not guaranteeing 'sufficient control of foreign adoption agencies regarding documentation required for adoption [and] undue payment.'[87]

66. Experience shows that the involvement of AABs of the receiving States in the intercountry adoption process can make a positive contribution to promoting the rights of the child deprived of a family, to respecting the principle of subsidiarity of intercountry adoption, as well as to providing multidisciplinary support, at various stages, to the children, the parents of

---

[84] Art. 11 of THC-1993: 'An accredited body shall a) pursue only non-profit objectives according to such conditions and within such limits as may be established by the competent authorities of the State of accreditation; b) be directed and staffed by persons qualified by their ethical standards and by training or experience to work in the field of intercountry adoption; and c) be subject to supervision by competent authorities of that State as to its composition, operation and financial situation.

[85] CRC Committee, *Concluding Observations: France* (UN Doc. CRC/C/15/Add.240, 2004), para. 33; *Albania* (UN Doc. CRC/C/15/Add.249, 2005), para. 47.

[86] CRC Committee, *Concluding Observations: Russian Federation* (UN Doc. CRC/C/15/Add.274, 2005), para. 42.

[87] *Ibid.*

origin and the adopters. The AABs' mediation thus increases the chances of a successful adoption and serves as an ethical guarantee. Nonetheless, this safeguard is not automatic. Indeed, numerous private AABs, sometimes accredited in their own State, have never given serious consideration to what, in their practice, the ethics of the best interests of the child mean. Some have been or are accomplices and sometimes protagonists in exerting pressure, in abusing, in violating the rights of the child, or even in trafficking. Furthermore, the number and the profile of AABs authorized to collaborate with a State of origin often take no account of children's needs and from the outset become a source of competition and pressure.

67. The mediation of an AAB in a receiving State is only a safeguard if it fulfils a certain number of requirements. Preferably an AAB should dispose of medical, psychosocial and legal professional competences as well as sufficient human and material resources to assume its responsibilities. The messages it conveys and its practice should reflect and prove its understanding of the ethics in adoption matters. It should have a sound knowledge of the entire machinery of adoption, of the profile of the children in need of intercountry adoption as well as of the family and child policy in the country of origin with which it is co-operating. Transparency in its links with other partners who could influence its activities and transparent financial management are also essential. Respect for these conditions presupposes, on the part of the concerned receiving States and States of origin, regular supervision of the AABs and a systematic review of the accreditations granted.

68. The nature of the involvement of an AAB in a specific country should be defined by both the receiving States and the States of origin. In order to respect the best interests of the child, the preliminary identification of the number and profile of the children in need of intercountry adoption is necessary, and, consequently, the number and profile of AABs should correspond. The authorities should, before taking any decision to approve or authorize an AAB, check that it responds to a real need and that it is not just attaching itself to an all too long list of AABs of various receiving States co-operating with the State of origin. Also, the tasks assigned to AABs by the receiving State and the State of origin have to be properly framed, according to its competences. Moreover, the AAB should guarantee, under the supervision of the receiving States and the States of origin, the ethics, the professionalism and the interdisciplinary nature of the intercountry adoption process. It plays the role of a close 'third party' and contributes to providing the necessary interventions and mediations by society and the State in defence of

children deprived of their family. The adoption body serves as a strong link between families, protagonists and authorities of receiving countries and of countries of origin.

69. Making it compulsory for prospective adopters to resort to an AAB of the receiving countries is now considered to be an important guarantee for intercountry adoptions.[88] In fact, the public authorities of the receiving countries and the countries of origin rarely have the material and human resources (trained and experienced interdisciplinary staff on site in sufficient number) to fully discharge the functions of preparing and supporting children, parents of origin and/or prospective adoptive parents.[89] And yet it is a matter of realizing an adoption procedure that complies, as far as possible, with the rights of the child and with the ethics advocated by international conventions. The role of the AAB thus depends upon a delegation by the States of a part of their duties to bodies in the private and/or public sector that correspond to the specific criteria set by law.[90] In addition, the obligation for the prospective adopters to resort to an AAB is part of the combat against certain abuses, trafficking and failures that stem from recourse to independent adoption. The CRC Committee in its recommendations to France, in May 2004, recalled the risks incurred by independent adoption, and encouraged recourse to an AAB.[91]

3.3.3 *Applicable Law and Procedure*

70. The involvement of 'competent authorities' in the adoption process is not sufficient in itself to ensure that this process is 'permissible' under Article 21 of the CRC. In accordance with the general principle of legality, the adoption of a child must be based on applicable law and procedures. This means that States Parties have an obligation to adopt and implement appropriate laws and procedures. The principle of the best interests of the child is not only a general rule which must prevail in any decision regarding adoption, but it should also be implemented through the adoption of appropriate legal and administrative measures. The CRC Committee particularly insisted on

---

[88] Some countries of origin (Bolivia, China, Ethiopia and India, for instance) and some receiving countries (Denmark, Finland, Norway, Sweden for instance) have made it compulsory to resort to an AAB.

[89] Arts. 12 and 21 of the CRC.

[90] This possibility is also foreseen by Article 22 of THC-1993.

[91] CRC Committee, *Concluding Observations: France* (UN Doc. CRC/C/15/Add.240, 2004), para. 33.

the States' responsibility to establish national statistics and comprehensive policy and guidelines on adoption.[92] Subsidiary regulatory instruments, as well as sufficient human and other resources, should also be made available to ensure the effective implementation of the Convention.[93] Finally, the Committee also deemed that mechanisms to review, monitor and follow up adoption procedures should be set up.[94] A complete policy and legislative framework is essential to guarantee full respect of the Convention. In this regard, the Committee has criticized the use of informal adoption, which may result in illegal practices.[95]

71. With regard to intercountry adoption, this obligation could be interpreted as requiring States Parties to the CRC to apply at least the basic guarantees of THC-1993. If, as some suggest, THC-1993 must be considered as "an implementing instrument of the CRC",[96] the implementation of Article 21 should be inspired by the provisions of the 1993 Convention. Some States have already included in their law and procedures parallel guarantees for intercountry adoptions which are governed by THC-1993 and those which are not (for example, some receiving States, which admit independent adoptions, systematically check the prospective adoptive parents' contact in the State of origin, even if the latter has not ratified THC-1993).

72. Regarding non-Hague adoptions, the States Parties to the CRC should be particularly attentive to the implementation of the subsidiarity principle, the checking of the adoptability of the child, the monitoring of possible independent adoptions, the combat against undue material gains, the co-operation between Central Authorities, the accreditation and authorization of intermediaries, the information of all parties, the checking of the suitability

---

[92] For example, in 2004, the CRC Committee recommended Brazil to 'collect in a systematic and on-going manner statistical data and relevant information on both domestic and intercountry adoption.' CRC Committee, *Concluding Observations: Brazil* (UN Doc. CRC/C/15/Add.241, 2004), para. 47. See also CRC Committee, *Concluding Observations: China* (UN Doc. CRC/C/CHN/CO/2, 2005), para. 52.

[93] CRC Committee, *Concluding Observations: France* (Un Doc. CRC/C/15/Add.240, 2004), para. 35; *Brazil,* (UN Doc. CRC/C/15/Add.241, 2004), para. 47; *Albania* (UN Doc. CRC/C/15/Add.249, 2005), para. 47.

[94] CRC Committee, *Concluding Observations: Armenia* (UN Doc. CRC/C/15/Add.119, 2000), paras. 30 and 31; *Kyrgyzstan* (UN Doc. CRC/C/15/Add.127, 2000), para. 38; *Tajikistan* (UN Doc. CRC/C/15/Add. 136, 2000), para. 33; *Brazil* (UN Doc. CRC/C/15/Add.241, 2004), para. 47.

[95] CRC Committee, *Concluding Observations: Liberia* (UN Doc. CRC/C/15/Add.236, 2004), para. 38; *Antigua and Barbuda* (UN Doc. CRC/C/15/Add.247, 2004), para. 45.

[96] J.H.A. van Loon, *l.c.* (note 9), p. 3.

of the prospective adoptive parents and the ban on all contacts between the latter and the parents or carers of the child before the matching decision.

3.3.4   Pertinent and Reliable Information

a) *Type of Information Required*

73. In order to meet the requirements of the principle of the best interests of the child and to comply with Article 21 of the CRC, each step of the adoption process must be based on relevant and reliable information (paragraph a). Information about the child should be gathered through psychological, medical, social and legal studies of the child and the birth family. The child's study must be as thorough as possible, since the child's future, that of his/her birth family, and that of the prospective adoptive family will depend upon it. The objectives of the study are to provide the clearest possible picture of the child and his/her family of origin – with their strengths and weaknesses, their individual and group resources and their limitations –, to assess the capacity of the family environment and to identify the child's needs. This should lead, as a priority, to the evaluation of the specific opportunities for maintaining the child in his/her family, or, if he/she is separated from it, to the preservation of his/her ties with the family and to a possible future reintegration in the family. It is only when such possibilities are impossible that adoption may be envisaged.[97]

74. As far as possible, the study, which is confidential, should cover:

- The identity of the child, his/her parents and extended family. If the child's parents are unknown, a search should be undertaken to trace them and discuss the child's future with them;
- The search of the child's birth family, comprising the immediate family (parents and siblings), and the extended family (grandparents, etc.). The socio-economic situation, the nature of relationships between relatives, the relationships with the social environment, the main difficulties and the positive factors are all elements of importance to evaluate the possibilities of uniting the child with his/her family members;
- The child's past, the stages of his/her personal and family history, ethnic and religious upbringing should be clearly exposed in as much detail as possible;

---

[97] On this issue, see ISS/IRC, *The rights of the child in domestic and intercountry adoption. Ethics and principles - Guidelines for practice*, 1999, revised 2004, p. 9. http://www.iss-ssi.org/Resource_Centre/Tronc_DI/tronc_di_eth.html.

– The reasons for the weakening or severance of the child's ties with the birth family, for the abandonment order, or the consent to adoption, have to be explained;
– The stages of the child's physical, motor, intellectual, and socio-emotional development should be detailed. His/her state of health, medical history (including available information about the mother's pregnancy and delivery, vaccinations, *etc.*) and that of the birth family are of importance too;
– His/her physical and general appearance, personality and behaviour should be described;
– The child's present situation, with all available information about his/her present environment, way of life, habits, ability to be self-reliant according to his/her age, relations with other children and adults around him/her, are also useful elements to guarantee as many answers as possible as the child grows up.[98]

75. Although Article 21 of the CRC only focuses in this paragraph on the adoptable child, State authorities must also base their decision on relevant and reliable information about prospective adoptive parents. This is the only way to ensure that the adoption foreseen in an individual case meets the best interests of the child. In intercountry adoption, THC-1993 requires that 'an adoption within the scope of the Convention shall take place only if the competent authorities of the receiving State have determined that the prospective adoptive parents are eligible and suited to adopt (Article 5 a)).

b) *Intercountry Adoption*

76. In intercountry adoption, countries of origin play a key role in the designation and establishment of authorities and procedures allowing appropriate information management. Their contribution is an important step forward in handling intercountry adoptions properly (and domestic adoptions as well). Clear identification of official interlocutors promotes the exchange of information and helps in solving problems. It also facilitates mutual understanding of administrative and judicial systems and may help to simplify procedures.

77. Countries of origin bear some of the most important obligations dictated by the CRC. According to W. Duncan, 'there is no doubt that the main burden of regulating and controlling the process of intercountry adoption is placed on the authorities of the State of origin.'[99] Implementing measures

---

[98] *Ibid.*
[99] W. Duncan, 'Intercountry Adoption: Some Issues in Implementing and Supplementing the 1993 Hague Convention on Protection of Children and Co-operation in Respect of Intercountry

are crucial in ensuring that adoption is truly carried out in the best interests of the child. Many issues have to be addressed by the country of origin
to this end: the respect of the subsidiarity principle, the free and informed
consent of biological parents, the restricted contact between the latter and
prospective adoptive parents, *etc.* Additionally, it is crucial that States have
judicial and administrative authorities in place which are able to undertake
the necessary procedures, according to the law.

78. On the other side, the authorities of receiving countries have their own
obligations, such as coordination, information, monitoring, and control.
They have to be informed about the situation prevailing in the various countries of origin and to identify risks. They are also in charge of evaluating
prospective adoptive parents and, by doing so, provide guarantees regarding the future well-being of the child. Their responsibilities also include the
monitoring of their AABs and the follow-up of adopted children.

79. The practice of intercountry adoption clearly demonstrates that a con-
crete knowledge of the reality where proceedings take place is fundamental
to ensure transparency of, and respect for, legality. Meetings with authorities, visits of institutions, follow-up of procedures, are means that may help
to make such decisions. Additionally, such means may enable the authorities
to fully realize the conditions under which their counterparts are working,
the pressures that they have to cope with, as well as to gain perspective on
adoption matters. It is up to the authorities to decide whether or not adoption can take place in specific contexts, whether respecting children's rights
or not.[100] By gaining a good understanding of the working conditions of a
country of origin, it is possible that a receiving country may decide that the

---

Adoption', in: J. Doek, H. van Loon, P. Vlaardingerbroek (eds.), *Children on the Move. How to
Implement their Right to Family Life* (The Hague, Martinus Nijhoff Publishers, 1996), p. 75.

[100] For instance, in the United Kingdom, the *Children and Adoption Act 2006* (Part 2) makes
provision regarding the restriction of intercountry adoptions from countries where the
Secretary of State has reason to believe that it would be contrary to public policy to further
the bringing of children into the United Kingdom by British citizens. This applies equally
to adoptions from countries that are signatories to THC-1993 and those that are not. The
suspension is achieved through a declaration made by the Secretary of State, who must
also publish his/her reasons for making the declaration in relation to each restricted country and publish a list of restricted countries, to be kept under review and up to date. The
Permanent Bureau of the Hague Conference is consulted in the information and evidence
gathering process. The effect of the restriction is that the appropriate authority would no
longer take any steps in processing intercountry adoption cases from the restricted country,
although adoptions may be permitted to continue in exceptional cases. *Children and Adoption
Act 2006*, http://www.opsi.gov.uk/ACTS/acts2006/20060020.htm; *Children and Adoption Act 2006:
Explanatory Notes*, http://www.opsi.gov.uk/ACTS/en2006/2006en20.htm.

minimum guarantees are no longer provided for, and therefore, that it will prevent procedures from carrying on any further.

3.3.5   Child's Status

a) *Adoptability*

80. As provided by Article 21, paragraph a of the CRC, the permissibility of adoption must be determined 'in view of the child's status concerning parents, relatives and legal guardians.' In other words, competent authorities of the States Parties must decide whether each child concerned is 'adoptable.' Adoption is a personalized life plan for a child. Such a plan can be decided upon only after a preliminary psychological, medical, social and legal study of the child and his/her birth family. The conclusion that it is impossible for the birth family to care for the child, and the assessment of the child's capacity to benefit from a family environment, determine his/her psycho-social adoptability. This is supplemented by his/her legal adoptability, which forms the basis for severance of the filiation links with birth parents, in the ways specified by the law of the State. The adoptability of the child must be determined before starting adoption proceedings and before a particular matching is considered, as foreseen by Article 4 b) of THC-1993.

81. Due to earlier experiences, some children may lose the ability or desire to develop a new bond of close emotional dependency, or they may show clear limitations in adjusting to a family environment. In this regard, it is of utmost importance that their psychological adoptability is properly assessed in order to try to avoid failures, and that adequate psychological support is provided to the children to be adopted in order for them to be prepared for their departure from their usual environment, in which they have established social and emotional ties.[101]

82. Adoptability may also be linked with the socio-political situation of the country of origin. Adoption is not a step to consider in countries where there is suspicion of corruption and trafficking, where armed conflict prevails or among victims of natural disasters. In the latter contexts, it may only be contemplated after a sufficient period (two years are generally recommended) to allow the competent bodies to ensure that no member of the child's family or community is still alive and is able and wishes to care for the child. Meanwhile, priority must be given to placing the child in a safe location, to

---

[101] ECtHR, *Pini, Bertani, Manera and Atripaldi v. Romania*, o.c. (note 25), para. 163.

in situ assistance measures in order to enable the child to remain in his/her community, and in his/her country or region if possible. For example, in the aftermath of the tsunami crisis in Asia, at the end of 2004, the international community took a clear position in banning international adoption in the affected areas.[102]

83. Refugee children are subject to specific protection too. According to UNHCR,[103] intercountry adoption for a refugee child should not be considered until his/her family situation is completely clear. In general, a two-year period is necessary to carry out a proper search for the biological family, but this may vary upon circumstances (for instance, if there are no longer any doubts about the child's status). The Hague Conference has also issued recommendations on this issue.[104]

b) *Children with Special Needs*
84. In every country, developing, in transition, or industrialized, the present challenge posed by adoption – both domestic and intercountry – and an important part of its future undoubtedly reside in the search for suitable families for children with special needs, as well as in suitably adapted professional practices.[105] Millions of children and young people 'with special needs' or 'who present particularities' reportedly live in family or institutional placements around the world. Also, it appears that very significant numbers of children are placed in institutions essentially because of their disability, even though it may be minor. The situation of the growing number of children affected by HIV/AIDS and living in institutions is a major concern too. The 'special needs label' may cover various situations, such as older children, carriers of a disease, a trauma or a handicap, children who have been in placement for a long time, or who belong to a sibling group that may not be split up. Too often, no permanency planning has been drawn up for them. Even if adoption is probably not the solution for the adequate

---

[102] See also the Hague Conference press release on this issue: 'Asian-African Tsunami Disaster and the Legal Protection of Children', 10 January 2005 http://www.hcch.net/index_en.php?act=publications.details&pid=3311&dtid=28.

[103] UNHCR *Refugee children: Guidelines on protection and care* 1994. Online. UNHCR Refworld, available at: http://www.unhcr.org/cgi-bin/texis/vtx/refworld/rwmain?docid=3ae6b3470

[104] Hague Conference on Private International Law, *Report of the Working Group of April 1994 to study the application to refugee children of the Hague Convention of 29 May 1993 on Protection of Children and Co-operation in respect of Intercountry Adoption* http://www.hcch.net/index_en.php?act=conventions.publications&dtid=2&cid=69.

[105] For further details on these practices, see ISS/IRC Monthly Review no 67, May 2004, Editorial, http://www.iss-ssi.org.

permanent protection of each of them, a certain number can be declared psycho-socially and legally adoptable. But depending upon the definition of 'special needs', that varies from country to country, some children differ much less from the profile of the child dreamed of by the prospective adopters: children just three years old, either carrying a harmless curable disease or handicap, who have lived through a trouble-free placement, or a sibling group of two healthy young children, *etc.* To classify these children in the category of 'children with special needs' no doubt sometimes unduly diminishes their chances of being adopted, when they could be integrated in a family, probably by means of professional support. At the global level, unlike the healthy young children the prospective adoptive parents are often waiting for – and will have to wait for increasingly longer and to no avail – children with special needs are waiting for families, in vain in most cases. The task of putting the requests of would-be adoptive parents in proper perspective necessarily presupposes a full awareness of the reality of children in need of adoption, in every country, on the part of the press, those in government, professionals and the public at large. Together with this awareness raising, professional practices should include information for prospective adoptive parents, before their suitability is judged, about the reality of children in need of domestic and intercountry adoption, together with an active search for prospective adopters likely to respond to the special needs of children.

3.3.6 *Informed Consent and Counselling*

85. The CRC grants some margin of manoeuvring to States Parties regarding the necessity to obtain the consent of all concerned before authorizing an adoption. This consent must be sought 'if required', meaning that it is up to domestic legislation whether or not to provide for this obligation. However, the lack of consent of some interested persons may infringe other provisions of the CRC or other human rights instruments, including the child's or birth parents' rights to family life,[106] or the child's right to be heard.[107] As reminded by UNICEF, '[c]hildren's ascertainable view must be central to any consideration of their "best interests."'[108] This fundamental principle was emphasized several times by the CRC Committee regarding domestic legislation on adoption. With regard to the situation in Germany in 1995,

---

[106] Arts. 7 and 9 of the CRC. See R. Hodgkin and P. Newell, *o.c.* (note 21), p. 298.
[107] Art. 12 of the CRC.
[108] R. Hodgkin and P. Newell, *o.c.* (note 21), p. 298.

for example, the Committee recommended that 'consideration be given to extending and broadening the involvement of children in decisions affecting them in the family and in social life, including in proceedings relating to family reunification and *adoption*.'[109]

86. In addition, not only the lack of consent, but also the way consent is given in some situations may be problematic under the Convention. The CRC Committee deems, for example, that States Parties should not authorize the parents to consent to the placement of their child up for adoption before birth.[110] It has also emphasized that the period of time after birth during which the mother may withdraw her consent should not be too short.[111] In all cases, appropriate counselling and support must be provided to all concerned.

87. In this regard, the European Court of Human Rights considered that the birth parents' right to be heard should imply access to relevant information, *i.e.* 'information which is relied on by the authorities in taking measures of protective care or in taking decisions relevant to the care and custody of a child',[112] and the right to legal representation during the care proceedings and the freeing for adoption proceedings.[113] In addition, the parents must also enjoy a real lapse of time between the two procedures for the hearing in court to be fair and effective.[114] Due process guarantees must also be respected.[115]

In the framework of intercountry adoption, the principle of participation of all concerned in the adoption process is also clearly confirmed and further detailed by THC-1993. This instrument defines the conditions under which consent in intercountry adoption may be considered as valid. Art. 4 c) and d) of this Convention states that:

> An adoption within the scope of the Convention shall take place only if the competent authorities of the State of origin [...]

---

[109] CRC Committee, *Concluding Observations: Germany* (UN Doc. CRC/C/15/Add. 43, 1995), para. 29 (emphasis added). See also CRC Committee, *Concluding Observations: Honduras* (UN Doc. CRC/C/15/Add.24, 1994), para. 26; *Mexico* (UN Doc. CRC/C/15/Add. 13, 1994), para. 18.

[110] CRC Committee, *Concluding Observations: Hungary* (UN Doc. CRC/C/HUN/CO/2/Add.244, 2006), paras. 17 and 33.

[111] *Ibid.*, para. 34.

[112] ECtHR, *P., C. and S. v. UK*, 56547/00, *o.c.* (note 28), para. 120.

[113] *Ibid.*, para. 137.

[114] *Ibid.*

[115] For further details, see I. Lammerant, *o.c.* (note 30), p. 43 *et seq.*

    c) have ensured that
        1) the persons, institutions and authorities whose consent is necessary for adoption, have been counselled as may be necessary and duly informed of the effects of their consent, in particular whether or not an adoption will result in the termination of the legal relationship between the child and his or her family of origin,
        2) such persons, institutions and authorities have given their consent freely, in the required legal form, and expressed or evidenced in writing,
        3) the consents have not been induced by payment or compensation of any kind and have not been withdrawn, and
        4) the consent of the mother, where required, has been given only after the birth of the child; and

    d) have ensured, having regard to the age and degree of maturity of the child, that
        5) he or she has been counselled and duly informed of the effects of the adoption and of his or her consent to the adoption, where such consent is required,
        6) consideration has been given to the child's wishes and opinions,
        7) the child's consent to the adoption, where such consent is required, has been given freely, in the required legal form, and expressed or evidenced in writing, and
        8) such consent has not been induced by payment or compensation of any kind.

88. Some of these rights are a matter for discussion because they may imply a conflict between the family of origin's interests and rights and those of the child. How to deal, for example, with a refusal to consent to adoption while, in fact, the child will be brought up in a life of upheaval and abandonment? As a matter of principle, adoption must only take place if the parents of origin have consented to it. However, there may be exceptional circumstances, restrictively defined by law, in which adoption without the consent of the parents may be contemplated or when the parents' right to consent to adoption may be denied, such as when the parents are dead, unknown or untraceable as well as when a forced adoption is necessary in the best interests of the child (unreasonable denial to consent to adoption, declaration of abandonment, when all efforts to work with the parents and to reintegrate the child have failed or proved ineffective, *etc.*).

89. If these questions are still difficult to answer, it is also because the general perception of adoption tends to overlook the individual origin of the child. By assuming that the child will have a better life in an adoptive family, in the case of intercountry adoption, in a Western country, the public may assimilate its general perception of a country of origin, generally considered as lacking adequate socio-economical infrastracture, with the situation of

every child and their family living there. This reaction is wrong and more explanations are needed to combat it. Children are part of their natural environment, together with their nuclear and extended family, their friends and neighbourhood. Even under difficult circumstances, children have their roots and a primary right to stay in their birth context. Any attempt of 'transplantation' has to be carried out with great consideration of the original environment.[116]

3.3.7 Abuses

90. Both national and intercountry adoption may give way to innumerable abuses and non-professional practices. Concern about such problems was particularly raised in relation to intercountry adoption. On various occasions, the CRC Committee has expressed concern both about the absence of a normative framework and illegal practices in the field of intercountry adoption. It has also insisted on the States' responsibility to set up mechanisms empowered to efficiently prevent and combat such violations of the Convention.[117] In the case of Guatemala, for example, the Committee was concerned 'at the extremely high rates of intercountry adoptions, at adoption procedures not requiring authorization by competent authorities, at the absence of follow-up and, in particular, at reported information on sale and trafficking in children for intercountry adoptions.'[118] As a result, it strongly recommended 'that the State party suspend adoptions in order to take the adequate legislative and institutional measures to prevent the sale and trafficking of children and to establish an adoption procedure which is in full compliance with the principles and provisions of the Convention.'[119]

---

[116] See also: ATD Fourth World, 'How poverty separates parents and children: a challenge to human rights', 2005, http://www.atd-uk.org/publications/Pub.htm. 'In the face of poverty, parents can show unstinting resilience and courage on behalf of their children, making enormous efforts to safeguard relation-ships and keep the family together. This study shows what ATD Fourth World has learnt about the fight against poverty from its grassroots action with families, and from that of other NGOs, in the Philippines, Burkina Faso, Haiti, Guatemala, the United Kingdom and the United States.'

[117] See CRC Committee, *Concluding Observations: Paraguay* (UN Doc. CRC/C/15/Add.166, 2006), para. 4, and (UN Doc. CRC/C/15/Add. 27, 1994), para. 11; *Nicaragua* (UN Doc. CRC/C/15/Add. 36, 1995), para. 18; *Ukraine* (UN Doc. CRC/C/15/Add. 42, 1995), para. 11; *Panama* (UN Doc. CRC/C/15/Add.233, 2004), para. 37.

[118] CRC Committee, *Concluding Observations: Guatemala* (UN Doc. CRC/C/15/Add.154, 2001), para. 34.

[119] *Ibid.*, para. 35.

91. The same concern also explains why Argentina entered a reservation on Articles 21 b) to e) of the CRC on intercountry adoption. This country argued that these subparagraphs could not apply within its jurisdiction, 'because, in its view, before they can be applied a strict mechanism must exist for the legal protection of children in matters of intercountry adoption, in order to prevent trafficking in and the sale of children.'[120] However, the CRC Committee did not share this argument and recommended Argentina to withdraw this reservation.[121]

92. As mentioned above,[122] States' obligation to combat illegal practices in intercountry adoption has also been recognized in the Optional Protocol on the Sale of Children, Child Prostitution and Child Pornography. In relation to adoption, trafficking means that the required procedures have not been fully followed and the child has been declared adoptable without due cause. For example, even though the adoption has been approved by a judge, this decision was based on a process which was not in compliance with legal requirements. However, this practice is not necessarily aimed at exploiting the child. Therefore it is important to distinguish systematically between children 'trafficked for the purpose of adoption,' and children supposedly 'trafficked through adoption for subsequent exploitation.'[123] Only on

---

[120] UN Treaty Collection, *Reservations and Declarations to the UN Convention on the Rights of the Child*, o.c. (note 6).

[121] CRC Committee, *Concluding Observations: Argentina* (UN Doc. CRC/C/15/Add.187, 2002), para. 13.

[122] *Cf. supra* (note 48).

[123] According to Art. 3 a) of the *UN Protocol to Prevent, Suppress and Punish Trafficking in Persons Especially Women and Children* (Palermo Protocol), trafficking means the recruitment, transportation, transfer, harbouring or receipt of persons, through various illegal practices, for the purpose of exploitation. Thus, for an act to be qualified as 'trafficking' under this Protocol, it must be shown to have an exploitative aim, defined as including, at a minimum, the exploitation of prostitution or other forms of sexual exploitation, forced labour or services, slavery, servitude or removal of organs. United Nations, UN Protocol to Prevent, Suppress and Punish Trafficking in Persons Especially Women and Children, supplementing the UN Convention against Transnational Organized Crime, adopted on 15 November 2000, not entered into force yet, http://www.ohchr.org/english/law/protocoltraffic.htm.
However, the CRC has a broader approach, as no exploitative aim is necessary for an act to be qualified as 'trafficking' (Art. 35 of the CRC). Under the terms of the CRC, then, trafficking can also be deemed to take place for a legal purpose such as adoption. In this sense, see also the 1994 *Inter-American Convention on International Traffic in Minors* whereby, for an act to be qualified as trafficking, its purpose does not have to be illegal if the means used are unlawful. Art. 2: 'International traffic in minors' means the abduction, removal or retention, or attempted abduction, removal or retention, for unlawful purposes (*prostitution, sexual exploitation, servitude*) or by unlawful means (*kidnapping, fraudulent or coerced consent, the giving or receipt of unlawful payments or benefits to achieve the consent of the parents, persons or institution having care of the child*). Organization of American States, Inter-American Convention on

that basis can the real problems be targeted in the fight against illegal and unprofessional practices in the adoption process.[124]

3.4   Intercountry Adoption as an Alternative Means of Child Care
(Art. 21, para. b)

3.4.1   Historical Background

93. Article 21, paragraph b of the CRC is based on a text submitted by the Dutch delegation during the second reading in 1989. This proposal was very similar to Article 17 of the 1986 UN Declaration.[125] This original version was adopted by the Working Group without major changes and thus is very similar to the final wording of the Convention.[126] By providing that intercountry adoption can be envisaged only when no other 'suitable' alternative measure is available to the child concerned in his/her country of origin, this paragraph enshrines the principle of subsidiarity of intercountry adoption. The text, however, was strongly criticized by the delegation of Venezuela. Its representative argued that intercountry adoption was 'an extreme and exceptional measure and, as such, should not be considered as 'an alternative means of child's care.'[127]

3.4.2   Subsidiarity of Intercountry Adoption

a) *Legal Perspectives*
94. Both the CRC and THC-1993 propose criteria that should be applied when identifying the best care solution for children deprived of their parents. Among these criteria, both instruments recognize that intercountry

---

International Traffic in Minors, adopted on 18 March 1994, entered into force on 15 August 1997, http://www.oas.org/juridico/English/sigs/b-57.html.

[124] N. Cantwell, "Is intercountry adoption linked with trafficking for exploitation?" ISS-IRC Monthly review, Editorial, No. 10–11 2005.

[125] This Article provides that 'if a child cannot be placed in a foster or an adoptive family or cannot in any suitable manner be cared for in the country of origin, intercountry adoption may be considered as an alternative means of providing the child with a family.'

[126] *Travaux Préparatoires* (UN Doc. E/CN.4/1989/WG.1/WP.45), reproduced in United Nations Centre for Human Rights, *o.c.* (note 5), p. 21.

[127] *Travaux Préparatoires* (UN Doc. E/CN.4/1989/48), reproduced in United Nations Centre for Human Rights, *o.c.* (note 5), p. 24, para. 356. See also the intervention by Canada, which stated that 'in any consideration of alternative family care, due regard should be paid to the desirability of continuity in a child's upbringing and to the child's ethnic, religious, cultural and linguistic background.' *Ibid.*, para. 368. And Brazil, which considered that this provision should be interpreted 'in the sense that intercountry adoption will only be envisaged as an alternative means of child care, when all possibilities are exhausted.' *Ibid.*, para. 369.

adoption may be envisaged only for children, for whom a suitable alternative form of care cannot be found in their country of origin, thus being the last solution.

95. The wording of Article 21, paragraph b of the CRC is particularly strict in this regard, providing that intercountry adoption may be considered only if the child 'cannot in any suitable manner be cared for in [his/her] country of origin.' As expressed by the CRC Committee in its final observations on the situation in Mexico, this principle means, in other words, that 'intercountry adoption should be considered, in the light of Article 21, namely as a measure of last resort.'[128] This is consonant with Article 20(3) of the CRC, which requires that, when considering solutions for alternative care, including adoption, 'due regard shall be paid to the desirability of continuity in a child's upbringing and to the child's ethnic, religious, cultural and linguistic background.' This means also that States Parties should implement measures aimed at promoting domestic suitable solutions, including adoption, before contemplating intercountry adoption.[129]

96. However, regarding this question, THC-1993 seems to allow for more flexibility. It requires States of origin to ensure that possibilities for placement of the child in their territory be given 'due consideration', before envisaging intercountry adoption for the child.[130] Moreover, it recognizes that intercountry adoption may constitute an alternative solution, when a 'suitable family' cannot be found in the State of origin.[131] While Article 21 of the CRC establishes the principle of subsidiarity of intercountry adoption over any other suitable alternative care in the child's country of origin, THC-1993 limits this principle to domestic family measures. Therefore, non family alternative care, such as residential care, should not prevail over intercountry adoption under THC-1993.[132]

---

[128] CRC Committee, *Concluding Observations: Mexico* (UN Doc. CRC/C/15/Add.13, 1994), para. 18. See also CRC Committee, *Concluding Observations: Brazil* (UN Doc. CRC/C/15/Add.241, 2004), para. 47; *Nicaragua* (UN Doc. CRC/C/15/Add.265, 2005), para. 39; *China* (UN Doc. CRC/C/CHN/CO/2, 2005), para. 53. See also Art. 24 b) of the *African Charter on the Rights and Welfare of the Child,* which explicitly provides that intercountry adoption may be considered as an alternative means of child's care 'as a last resort.' African Union, African Charter on the Rights and Welfare of the Child, *o.c.* (note 19).

[129] CRC Committee, *Concluding Observations: Russian Federation* (UN Doc. CRC/C/15/Add.274, 2005), para. 4.

[130] Art. 4 b) of THC-1993.

[131] Preamble of THC-1993.

[132] On this difference between the CRC and THC-1993, see S. Dillon, 'Making Legal Regimes for Intercountry Adoption Reflect Human Rights Principles: Transforming the United Nations

b) *Other Forms of Subsidiarity*

97. This criterion, however, must be balanced with other principles, which are also rooted in international instruments and which add other dimensions to the notion of subsidiarity. Both the CRC and THC-1993 consider that family solutions (return to the birth family, foster care, adoption) should generally be preferred to institutional placement.[133] According to the most widespread interpretation, birth family, in this context, consists largely of father and mother, and failing that, as long as it is in the child's interest, other members of the family liable to take the child into their care.

98. If, in certain special cases, long term placement in an institution may seem to meet the best interests of the child (certain children, given the traumas they have experienced or given particular personal characteristics, are unable or unwilling to reinsert themselves in their family of origin or in an adoptive family), it is nonetheless accepted at the international level that, essentially, it is in the best interests of the child to be raised in a family environment that ensures him/her permanence and individualized attention. It is certain that adoption – domestic and intercountry – will only be a life plan for a limited number of children. But this option must be offered to them by the laws and by the professionals when it corresponds to their best interests. This measure must have its place in the range of responses offered in the framework of a deinstitutionalization policy, on condition, of course, that it is hedged with the indispensable guarantees and accepted by the legal and cultural context.

99. Another component of the principle of subsidiarity is that permanent solutions (return to the birth family, adoption) should in principle be preferred to provisional ones (institutional placement, foster care). This results notably from Article 20(3) of the CRC, which requires that 'due regard shall be paid to the desirability of continuity in a child's upbringing', when considering alternative care.[134] In certain situations, however, institutional placement or foster care can constitute the most suitable permanent solution for a child. As a general rule, when the child cannot live with his/her

---

Convention on the Rights of the Child with the Hague Convention on Intercountry Adoption', *Boston University International Law Journal* 21, 2003, pp. 208–215; L. Kaufmann, 'Memorandum presented by the Centre for Adoption Policy Studies', http://www.adoptionpolicy.org/pdf/hague.pdf.

[133] See notably the Preambles of both conventions.

[134] On these various aspects of the principle of subsidiarity, see UNICEF, *Innocenti Digest No. 4. Intercountry Adoption, o.c.* (note 1), p. 5.

father and mother, both the reality of the ties, which he/she has really lived through or experienced with regard to them, and his/her need for new filiation attachment ties in the form of adoption, must be taken into account in order to determine the most suitable solution for him/her. Unlike adoption, placement must be subjected to periodic review (Article 25 of the CRC).

c) *Implementation*

100. Sometimes these various principles contradict each other. What happens, for example, when a child without parents has a chance of either being placed with an aunt outside the country or in an unrelated family living in his/her own country? Does priority have to be given to the child's family ties abroad or to the continuity of his/her education, as well as ethnic, religious, cultural and linguistic origins? Consequently should the child be placed with the aunt, running the risk of creating in him/her a sense of being uprooted, and putting his/her emotional development in jeopardy, or would it be preferable to choose a domestic solution, to the detriment of his/her family ties? This situation raises the question of the place allotted to the extended family as caregivers within the range of care measures for children deprived of their family. Implicitly, it also raises the question of the means of harmonising the priority to the family of origin and the principle of subsidiarity, when they risk leading to incompatible solutions.

101. It is vital to recall here that this dilemma should not be solved in the abstract in absolute fashion. Each specific case should be studied individually, so as to devise a permanency planning in keeping with the principle of the child's best interests. It is a matter, first of all, of taking into consideration all the personal characteristics of the child (his/her history and that of the family, his/her age, the state of physical and mental health, the nature of his/her current family relations and friendships, religion, cultural bonds, adaptive capacities, *etc.*). To the extent possible, it is also desirable to take into account the views of the child as well as those of the father and mother, if possible, and to prepare the child for the solution agreed upon. Finally the characteristics of the potential care environment must be assessed. This means, particularly, to assess how the child will be integrated in the family, the social group and the society where he/she will be placed. It also means to bear in mind the alternative solution which was not chosen. In other words, it entails proceeding to weighing up the interests with a view to identifying the solution that best responds to the child's needs.

3.5   The Principle of Non-Discrimination (Art. 21, para. c)

3.5.1   Historical Background

102. As previously mentioned, the principle of non-discrimination in inter-country adoption was among the first amendments proposed on the draft convention submitted by Poland in 1978. This proposal, which was presented by Colombia,[135] intended to oblige States Parties to recognize 'the same rights' to children adopted by foreigners and to children of the country in which they would be adopted. However, some delegations raised concern about this draft provision, arguing that such an obligation was too strict and would be difficult to implement in practice. An alternative text was thus submitted, according to which States Parties would be bound to applying 'equivalent' safeguards and standards to both groups of children and would have to do it only 'to the maximum extent possible.'[136] This last formula was supported by Norway, which, in addition, expressed its doubts about the States' capacity to 'ensure' that the principle of non-discrimination could be respected in all situations. However, the suggestion to adopt a lighter choice of wording on this point was eventually rejected by the Working Group.

103. The final wording of the non-discrimination principle in the CRC is similar to Article 20 of the 1986 UN Declaration. This provision states that '[i]n intercountry adoption, placements should, as a rule, be made through competent authorities or agencies with application of safeguards and standards equivalent to those existing in respect of national adoption.' However, the text of the CRC appears to be stronger, since it recognizes the child's direct ownership of the safeguards and standards.

3.5.2   Legal Framework

104. While the principle of non-discrimination is focused on intercountry adoption in Article 21 of the CRC, it is clear that it also applies to domestic procedures. The prohibition of discrimination is a general human right based on customary law as well as various international conventions[137] and applies,

---

[135] *Travaux Préparatoires* (UN Doc. E/CN.4/1324/Add.2), reproduced in United Nations Centre for Human Rights, *o.c.* (note 5), p. 5.

[136] *Travaux Préparatoires* (UN Doc. E/CN.4/1989/WG.1/WP.45), reproduced in United Nations Centre for Human Rights, *o.c.* (note 5), p. 21; and *Travaux Préparatoires* (UN Doc. E/CN.4/1989/WG.1/WP.62), reproduced in United Nations Centre for Human Rights, *o.c.* (note 5), p. 23.

[137] At the universal level, see Art. 2(2) of the CESCR and Art. 2(1) of the CCPR.

as such, to any child concerned by adoption.[138] As a general principle, the CRC also provides that States Parties must implement its provisions 'without discrimination of any kind, irrespective of the child's or his or her parent's or legal guardian's race, colour, sex, language, religion, political or other opinion, national, ethnic or social origin, property, disability, birth or other status.'[139] With regard to the situation in Hungary in 2006, for example, the CRC Committee was concerned by the high number of Roma children in institutions who did not benefit from adoption.[140]

105. Nonetheless, this principle does not exclude all distinction between individuals. Only those which are not based on legitimate grounds are prohibited. It may even be that the obligation of non-discrimination imposes the creation of advantages for certain categories of persons in compensating for the social imbalances that are at the root of inequalities. The principle envisaged here therefore, by virtue of its very generality, must be specified according to the fields in which it needs to be applied. In matters of adoption, its implications are manifold and call for shades of meaning.

3.5.3   Implementation

a) Domestic / Intercountry Adoption

106. The CRC stresses the risk of inequalities that may be linked to the distinction between domestic and intercountry adoption. It prescribes that States Parties must ensure, 'that the child concerned by intercountry adoption enjoys safeguards and standards equivalent to those existing in the case of national adoption' (Art. 21, para. c). Practice shows, however, that the opposite hypothesis must be envisaged with just as much, if not greater, attention, for example when traditional kinship care is common. It often happens, in fact, that the safeguards granted by domestic adoption procedures do not achieve the level of protection foreseen by intercountry adoption. While, therefore, Article 21, paragraph c of the CRC retains all of its relevance, it is also essential to recall that the States also bear responsibility for ensuring that children adopted in their own country benefit, particularly, from legal and psychosocial guarantees (intervention of qualified and supervised professionals, checking the child's adoptability and the

---

[138] R. Hodgkin and P. Newell, *o.c.* (note 21), p. 296.
[139] Art. 2(1) of the CRC.
[140] CRC Committee, *Concluding Observations: Hungary* (UN Doc. CRC/C/HUN/CO/2/Add.244, 2006), para. 34.

suitability of the prospective adoptive parents, preparing the child and the parents, professional matching, post-adoption support) equivalent to those provided in intercountry adoption.

b) *Intercountry Adoption within / outside the Framework of the Hague Convention of 1993*
107. Since THC-1993, like all international treaties, is only binding for Member States, the way intercountry adoption procedures function risks being different depending upon whether or not the States concerned are parties to the Convention. If they are not, basic guarantees may not be applied to the detriment of the child's best interests.[141] As an example, some receiving States Parties allow their habitual residents to undertake direct adoptions which do not respect the guarantees provided by Article 29 of THC-1993 – thus bargaining directly with the child's parents or guardian in non-States Parties, although other receiving States Parties prohibit such adoptions.

108. In respecting the interests of each child, it is for the receiving States that have subscribed to THC-1993 to offer the same fundamental guarantees to all children, whether they hail from a country of origin that is a party to the Convention or not. In the same way, it is for the States of origin that are parties to THC-1993 to offer the same guarantees to all children, be they adopted in a receiving country party to the Convention or not. When a non-party State is unable to furnish such guarantees on its own, they must be implemented jointly by the AABs, their representatives and their local partners. In this case, the level of involvement, the demands made, the support and supervision by the State Party to the Convention must be particularly high in relation to the accreditation and authorization of adoption bodies.

109. Some major intergovernmental bodies have already expressed this concern. In its 2 December 1999 report, the Parliamentary Assembly of the Council of Europe 'calls on the Committee of Ministers of the Council of Europe to give a clear indication of its political will to ensure that children's rights are respected, by immediately inviting the Member States to ratify the Hague Convention on Adoption if they have not already done so, and undertake to observe its principles and rules even when dealing with countries that have not themselves ratified it.'[142] It also has to be recalled that the

---

[141] *Cf. supra* 3.3.3. Applicable Law and Procedure, for more details about the application of THC-1993 with non-contracting States.
[142] Council of Europe, Parliamentary Assembly, Social, Health and Family Affairs Committee, *International adoption: respecting children's rights* (Doc. 8592), 2 December 1999, http://assembly.

first Special Commission of the Hague Conference on intercountry adoption in 2000 recommended that States Parties 'as far as is practicable, apply the standards and safeguards of the Convention to the arrangements for intercountry adoption which they make in respect of non-Contracting States.'[143]

c) *Adoptions Resorting to an Accredited Adoption Body / Independent Adoption*
110. The choice of prospective adoptive parents whether or not to resort to an AAB can also be a factor of inequality between children. The accredited bodies, in particular, are guarantors, with and under the control of the States, of the existence, professionalism and the multidisciplinary nature of the medical, legal and psychosocial work undertaken (information, preparation, support) for the benefit of the child, the family of origin and the adoptive family. They assume the role of 'third party' on the spot, and carry out the necessary intervention and mediation of society and the State in protecting children deprived of their family. Even in this case, it is essential to be sure that the children involved in the adoption procedure enjoy the same rights, independently of the public or private status of the accredited body in question, especially, in case of intercountry adoption, regarding the professionalism and reliability of the intermediaries in the country of origin.

111. In the case of independent adoption – *i.e.* where no AAB intervenes – the role of the third party does not arise and respect for certain safeguards may be missing. However, where independent adoption is authorized – as is the case in many States – the latter must ensure that all the functions of an accredited body (including, in the case of intercountry adoption, checking the reliability and training of the intermediary in the country of origin) are accomplished, with the same safeguards, by the official bodies concerned.

d) *Non-Related / Relative Adoptions*
112. The principle of non-discrimination also requires that relative adoptions (of the child of the spouse or of a child related to at least one of the adopters) benefit as far as possible from the same level of guarantees as non-related adoptions. This is particularly important as regards the respect

---

coe.int//Mainf.asp?link=http://assembly.coe.int/Documents/WorkingDocs/doc99/EDOC8592.htm.
[143] Hague Conference on Private International Law, *Report and Conclusions of the Special Commission*, 2001, http://hcch.e-vision.nl/index_en.php?act=publications.details&pid=2273&dtid=2 or www.iss-ssi.org/Resource_Centre/Tronc_CI/reportspecom2000.PDF, para. 56, recommandation No. 11.

for the principle of subsidiarity and the search for the best interests of the child, the verification of the medical, psychological, social and legal adoptability of the child, as well as the verification of the suitability of the prospective adoptive parents, the preparation of all the interested parties and the follow-up to the situation. This is not systematically the case in current practice.

e) *Adoption of Children with Special Needs*
113. In the case of children 'with special needs', the principle of non-discrimination requires the adoption of specific (positive) measures. Here it is not a matter of avoiding an arbitrary distinction between the individuals concerned, but rather, on the contrary, of arranging measures in order for these children to receive specific treatment adapted to their 'special needs.'[144]

114. As demonstrated by the example of adoption, the principle of non-discrimination cannot be mechanically applied. It has to be adapted to each context. Depending on the cases, it requires either to identify differences of treatments which may not be justified under the best interests of the child or, on the contrary, to take specific measures aimed at compensating inequalities. Only this differentiated approach ensures that one child is equal to another in practice.

3.6   *Improper Financial Gain in Intercountry Adoption (Art. 21, para. d)*

3.6.1   *Historical Background*

115. The question of the cost of adoption was raised at the end of the drafting process of Article 21 of the CRC. A new paragraph prohibiting improper financial gain in intercountry adoption was added in 1989 by a group of States, which had been set up to focus on adoption and family issues in the elaboration of the Convention.[145] This paragraph was reproduced from Article 20 of the 1986 UN Declaration, which provides that '[i]n no case should the placement result in improper financial gain for those involved in it.' This amendment was strongly criticized by the delegation of Venezuela, which deemed that such a provision would promote trafficking. It was argued that

---

[144] *Cf. supra* No. 84.
[145] *Travaux Préparatoires* (UN Doc. E/CN.4/1989/48), reproduced in United Nations Centre for Human Rights, o.c. (note 5), p. 23, para. 349.

prohibiting 'improper' gain would imply that 'proper' gain was admissible and that this rule would contribute to the development of a 'market for children.'[146] Despite this opposition, the draft paragraph was finally adopted by the Working Group, and then by the UN General Assembly, without any change. Trafficking of children was to be dealt with under Article 35 of the CRC, which provides that 'States Parties shall take all appropriate national, bilateral and multilateral measures to prevent the abduction of, the sale of or traffic in children *for any purpose or in any form.*'[147] This includes the sale of or traffic in children for the purpose of adoption.

116. The rapid increase of funds raised in the context of intercountry adoption processes, coupled with the emerging trends of their commercialization, were amongst the concerns, raised particularly by NGOs and countries of origin, that gave way to the elaboration of THC-1993. Article 32 of this instrument specifies the prohibition of improper financial gain in the process of intercountry adoption, stating that 'only costs and expenses, including reasonable professional fees of persons involved in the adoption, may be charged or paid' and that 'the directors, administrators and employees of bodies involved in an adoption shall not receive remuneration which is unreasonably high in relation to services rendered.'[148]

117. However, there is reason to fear that financial abuses may continue to exist, not only in non-ratifying States, but also in States Parties to THC-1993. It does not always appear certain that all the authorities of the receiving States are in a position to effectively control the financial transactions of their accredited bodies or of their prospective adoptive parents in the States of origin. In the same way, not all of the Central Authorities of the States of origin are in the position to effectively control the financial transactions of their accredited bodies, those of the receiving States, those of the prospective adoptive parents or those of other persons intervening in the adoption process in their respective States.

3.6.2   *Implications*

118. A point of specific concern is the costs and fees involved in independent adoptions. It appears impossible to have any perception of the level of

---

[146] *Travaux Préparatoires* (UN Doc. E/CN.4/1989/48), reproduced in United Nations Centre for Human Rights, *o.c.* (note 5), p. 24, paras. 356 and 729.
[147] Emphasis added.
[148] Art 32(2) and (3) of THC-1993.

these costs and fees, or which parties are involved in these specific types of adoptions. Considering the emotional consequences associated with adoption for adopter and adoptee, as well as the real risks of abuse, this topic cannot be left to individual responsibility. In addition to these financial aspects, fundamental ethical issues, linked to the implementation of the CRC and THC-1993 are also a cause for concern when it comes to independent adoptions. This includes the risks of preventing the application of the subsidiarity principle, indirectly promoting the abandonment of children as well as infringing upon basic human rights.

119. Of course, any adoption process will procure some costs, for both governmental and non-governmental services. If reasonable fees are permitted, it is not easy to set a clear limit of what falls out of permissibility. As the Hague Conference does, one could divide the issue in four main categories:

> a) Structural funding: linking child protection programmes with adoption fees should be avoided as it may generate pressure on public servants and dependency in operating a sufficient number of adoptions per year;
> b) Usual administrative fees are normal, as long as they are reasonable and receiving States should know the rates. 'Rarely is the payment of official fees the problem. Most countries have reasonable fees for the processing of adoption';[149]
> c) Contribution, as a mean to support birth families, child protection services or institutions, is a more controversial issue. The following statement was proposed by the Special Commission of the Hague Conference: 'Receiving countries are encouraged to support efforts in countries of origin to improve national child protection services, including programmes for the prevention of abandonment. However, this support should not be offered or sought in a manner which compromises the integrity of the intercountry adoption process, or creates a dependency on income deriving from intercountry adoption. In addition, decisions concerning the placement of children for intercountry adoption should not be influenced by levels of payment or contribution. These should have no bearing on the possibility of a child being made available, nor on the age, health or any characteristic of the child to be adopted';[150]
> d) To be permitted, donations should not be in cash but through bank transfer, they should be notified to the authorities of the States of origin and receiving States and should be properly registered by the institution that receives them.

---

[149] Special Commission of The Hague Conference on Private International Law, *Draft Guide to Good Practice under the Hague Convention of 29 May 1993 on Protection of Children and Co-operation in Respect of Intercountry Adoption: Implementation*, September 2005, http://www.hcch.net/index_en.php?act=publications.details&pid=3657&dtid=2, p. 87.

[150] *Ibid.*, p. 88.

3.7 Bilateral and Multilateral Arrangements (Art. 21, para. e)

3.7.1 Historical Background

120. No particular debate took place, during the negotiations of the CRC, on the question of the development of Article 21 through bilateral or multilateral arrangements or agreements. A few speakers drew the attention of the Working Group to the fact that this 'basic idea' was missing in the first draft provision on intercountry adoption and the proposal to add this possibility was accepted without further discussion.[151] The compromise text elaborated by the Argentine, French and Norwegian delegations therefore proposed a new sentence inviting States or authorized agencies to conclude agreements.[152] During the last round of discussion, the representative of the Union of Soviet Socialist Republics deemed that this paragraph should be clarified by adding that such arrangements or agreements were meant to be 'international'. However, the Working Group took the view that this mention was not necessary, since this paragraph would concern only States Parties. The arrangements or agreements in question would thus be international by nature.[153]

121. The main international agreement on intercountry adoption is THC-1993. Its scope and purpose is broader than the issue envisaged in Article 21, paragraph e of the CRC. The CRC Committee regularly recommends States Parties to the Convention to ratify THC-1993.[154] When States Parties have not ratified THC-1993, the Committee may invite them to reach specific bilateral agreements on determined issues, such as the identification of the suitability of the prospective adoptive parents or post-adoption follow-up.[155]

---

[151] *Travaux Préparatoires, Report of the Working Group to the Commission on Human Rights* (UN Doc. E/CN.4/1982/30/Add.1), reproduced in United Nations Centre for Human Rights, *o.c.* (note 5), p. 12, para. 78.

[152] *Ibid.,* para. 79.

[153] *Travaux Préparatoires, Report of the Working Group to the Commission on Human Rights* (UN Doc. E/CN.4/1989/48), reproduced in United Nations Centre for Human Rights, *o.c.* (note 5), p. 28, para. 375.

[154] CRC Committee, *Concluding Observations: Armenia* (UN Doc. CRC/C/15/Add.119, 2000), para. 31; *Guatemala* (UN Doc. CRC/C/15/Add.154, 2001), para. 35; *Kyrgyzstan* (UN Doc. CRC/C/15/Add.244, 2004), para. 42; *Nicaragua* (UN Doc. CRC/C/15/Add.265,2005), para. 39.

[155] CRC Committee, *Concluding Observations: Russian Federation* (UN Doc. CRC/C/15/Add.274, 2005), para. 43.

3.7.2 Scope and Purpose of THC-1993

122. Amongst the greatest assets of THC-1993 are, as the name suggests, the promotion of the best interests and fundamental rights of children, and the creation of a co-operative system between States, through Central Authorities, competent authorities and AABs (Art. 1).

The co-operative system created by THC-1993 builds into each specific case of adoption *a joint responsibility* of the State of origin and the receiving State (through their authorities and bodies) in order to ensure that both the letter and the spirit of the CRC and THC-1993 be implemented, that is to say centred on children's needs and rights. Therefore, States Parties to the Convention agree that if children from one State need intercountry adoption, and if this State co-operates with other States Parties (which may be considered a safeguard), then the adoption has to be carried out according to the requirements protecting children and the co-operative system provided by the Convention.

123. Co-operation between State Parties can thus only be shaped by the best interests of the children concerned. However, some authorities and accredited bodies (especially in receiving States) seem to use this concept of co-operation in an effort to convince States of origin that they have to entrust adoptable children to them for non-relative intercountry adoption: supposedly, if both States are bound by THC-1993, States of origin would not be able to refuse offers of co-operation from receiving States. This allegation sometimes claims to be based on the traditional legal theory of treaties (the binding effect of treaties): should a State ratify or accede to a treaty, it commits itself to entering into relationships with the other States Parties. Some States of origin are thus reluctant to ratify or accede to the Convention, thinking that as States Parties, they would be obliged to co-operate with all other States Parties. However, this interpretation does not take into account the purpose of the Convention. The best interests of children cannot be interpreted to mean that every State has an obligation to accept files from prospective adoptive parents from the (currently) 68 other States Parties.

124. In particular, since the international situation clearly demonstrates that the number of young and healthy adoptable children is dwindling in many countries and many intercountry adoptable children have special needs (older children, siblings, children with health problems), it may be more in the interests of these children for a State of origin to co-operate with a restricted number of receiving States, and preferably AABs, which can pro-

pose files of prospective adoptive parents who precisely match the needs of the children. Several reasons based on the best interests of children can justify such a choice. A limited number of partners contribute to enhancing the specialization of foreign counterparts and to strengthening ties and thereby the expertise relating to the particular children concerned. Furthermore, it prevents States of origin from being overwhelmed by a disproportionate number of sometimes unsuitable requests from foreign prospective adoptive parents, which hinder their ability to focus on assessing the situation of children in care. In the best interests of children, a State of origin might also prefer to co-operate with States which have common linguistic, cultural or other specificities: this feeling of common characteristics can help professionals to build closer co-operation, and the adopted children to integrate their adoptive family and society more harmoniously, and thereafter to revert to their roots. States of origin can also decide to work by choice with States which share their values relating to child welfare: countries with compatible child welfare systems and similar professional and ethical standards for assessing the suitability and the preparation of prospective adoptive parents may indeed develop better and closer co-operation. Similar national languages may also make cooperation easier among some States.

3.7.3   *Other Arrangements*

125. In addition to the regional conventions already presented, some States have ratified specific agreements. Some have a very limited scope, for instance in regulating the channel of files between the two countries. However, and despite the explanations mentioned above, some States still prefer to collaborate on a bilateral basis, mainly with the aim of limiting the number of contracting States. Allowing a limited number of adoption agencies to operate in a country of origin may also be decided upon by both States involved. Of course, the content of any multi- or bilateral agreement has to be in full compliance with the content of the CRC. In other words, only implementing measures or broader guarantees as the ones provided by the CRC are to be considered in this context.

CHAPTER FOUR

CONCLUSION

126. Article 21 of the CRC, together with its interpretation by the CRC Committee, offers substantial protection to children concerned by national or intercountry adoption. However, some issues fall outside the scope of the Article and still need to be addressed. Firstly, before undertaking the adoption process, dissemination of good practices and explanations about the reality of children in need of adoption are crucial. Preparation of prospective adoptive parents in an attempt to respond to the needs of the countries of origin will also probably be unavoidable in the near future. Secondly, once the adoption is completed, the issue of the child's origin (search of origins, access to personal files or even contact with biological parents) deserves greater attention, especially as demands from adopted children have already begun to grow in numbers. As the CRC Committee has stated, adopted children have a right to know their original identity.[156] For this purpose, States are encouraged to establish appropriate procedures, including 'recommended age and professional support measures.'[157] There is also a need for authorities, psychosocial bodies and professionals to envisage and introduce post-adoption policies and services which foster respect for the rights of the child, of the adoptive family and of the family of origin. Such provisions are particularly indispensable in responding to the explicit requests for support from all concerned. These services also constitute essential tools in terms of prevention of adoption failures.

127. In a quite short period of time, the process of adoption has experienced significant improvement, especially due to the implementation of the CRC and THC-1993. If some abuses still exist, the efforts made by legislators, experts and society as a whole lead to a far better supervision which limits risks. However, one should not forget that adoption is only one measure in the

---

[156] CRC Committee, *Concluding Observations: Ukraine* (UN Doc. CRC/C/15/Add.191, 2002), para. 49; *Kyrgyzstan* (UN Doc. CRC/C/15/Add.244, 2004), para. 41; *China* (UN Doc. CRC/C/CHN/CO/2, 2005), para. 53; *Russian Federation* (UN Doc. CRC/C/15/Add.274, 2005), paras. 40 and 41; *Hungary* (UN Doc. CRC/C/HUN/CO/2, Add.244, 2006), para. 35.

[157] CRC Committee, *Concluding Observations: Russian Federation* (UN Doc. CRC/C/15/Add.274, 2005), para. 41.

protection of children, which should be carried out among a wider spectrum of provisions. Children enjoy fundamental rights, and priority must be given to allowing children to be raised in their own family, *i.e.* remaining with the birth parents or the extended family. Governments and civil society must do their utmost to ensure that families of origin have the possibility and are encouraged to care for their children.

BIBLIOGRAPHY

ATD Fourth World, 'How poverty separates parents and children: a challenge to human rights', 2005, http://www.atd-uk.org/publications/Pub.htm.

Bartner-Graff, N., 'Intercountry Adoption and the Convention on the Rights of the Child: Can the Free Market in Children be Controlled?', *Syracuse Journal of International Law* 27, 2000, 405–430.

Boéchat, H., *Adoption internationale: une évolution entre éthique et marché*, Geneva: Edition de la Fondation Suisse du Service Social International, 2006.

Cantwell, N., 'Intercountry Adoption. A Comment on the Number of "Adoptable" Children and the Number of Persons Seeking to Adopt Internationally', Hague Conference of Private International Law, '*The Judges' Newsletter*', Volume V – Spring 2003.

Detrick, S., *A commentary on the United Nations Convention on the Rights of the Child*, The Hague: Martinus Nijhoff Publishers, 1999.

——. (ed.), *The United Nations Convention on the Rights of the Child, A Guide to the "Travaux Préparatoires"*, The Hague: Martinus Nijhoff Publishers, 1992.

Dillon, S., 'Making Legal Regimes for Intercountry Adoption Reflect Human Rights Principles: Transforming the United Nations Convention on the Rights of the Child with the Hague Convention on Intercountry Adoption', *Boston University International Law Journal* 21, 2003, 179–257.

Duncan, W., 'Intercountry Adoption: Some Issues in Implementing and Supplementing the 1993 Hague Convention on Protection of Children and Co-operation in Respect of Intercountry Adoption', in: J. Doek, H. van Loon, P. Vlaardingerbroek (eds.), *Children on the Move. How to Implement their Right to Family Life*, The Hague: Martinus Nijhoff Publishers, 1996.

Hodgkin, R. and Newell, P., *Implementation Handbook for the Convention on the Rights of the Child*, second edition, New York: UNICEF, 2002.

ISS/IRC, *The rights of the child in intern and intercountry adoption. Ethics and principles guidelines for practice*; http://www.iss-ssi.org/Resource_Centre/Tronc_DI/tronc_di_eth.html.

Kilkelly, U., *The Child and the European Convention on Human Rights*, Dartmouth: Ashgate, 1999.

Lammerant, I., *L'adoption et les droits de l'homme en droit comparé*, Bruxelles: Bruylant, 2001.

Lücker-Babel, M.F., *Adoption internationale et droits de l'enfant*, Fribourg: Editions Universitaires, 1991.

——, *Adoption internationale: comprendre les nouvelles normes*, Geneva : Défense des Enfants-International, 1996.

——, 'Intercountry Adoption and Trafficking in Children: An Initial Assessment of the Adequacy of the International Protection of Children and their Rights', *International Review of Penal Law* 62, 1991, 799–818.

Parra-Aranguren, G., *Convention of 29 May 1993 on Protection of Children and Co-operation in respect of Intercountry Adoption: Explanatory Report*.

Saclier, C., International Social Service, *Understanding Children's Rights*. Collected papers presented at the second International Interdisciplinary Course on Children's Rights, University of Ghent (Belgium), July 1997, p. 701.

Smolin, D.M., 'Intercountry Adoption as Child Trafficking', *Valparaiso University Law Review* 39, 2004, 281–325.

UNICEF, *Innocenti Digest No. 4. Intercountry Adoption*, Florence: UNICEF ICDC, 1999.

United Nations Centre for Human Rights, *Legislative History of the Convention on the Rights of the Child (1978-1989), Article 21 (Adoption)*, HR/1995/Ser.1/Article 21.

Verdier, P., *L'enfant en miettes*, Toulouse: Privat, 1978.

Van Binh Nguyen, 'Le droit et la pratique de l'adoption internationale au Vietnam', in: Assocation Louis Chatin, *L'adoption internationale en droit comparé*, Actes du colloque, 25–26 April 2003.

Van Loon, J.H.A., 'International Co-operation and Protection of Children with regard to Intercountry Adoption', *RCADI* 244, 1993–VII, 195–456.